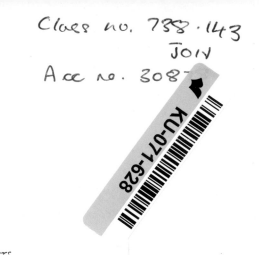

Ridge Danyers - Marple Site

M0030878

Raku – investigations into fire

RAKU
investigations into fire

David Jones

The Crowood Press

First published in 1999 by
The Crowood Press Ltd
Ramsbury, Marlborough
Wiltshire SN8 2HR

© David Jones 1999

Dedication
To my father, mother and Merlin and Rhiannon who have all taught me that through books one can start to understand the world.

British Library Cataloguing-in-Publication Data
A catalogue record for this book is available from the British Library.

ISBN 1 86126 139 X

Photograph previous page: 'Two totemic vessels' (28in/71cm), David Jones. (Photograph by Rod Dorling.)

Disclaimer
Kiln building and firing can be hazardous. If all health and safety instructions are followed carefully then Raku can be as safe and enjoyable an experience as any other ceramic activity. The author and the book publisher (The Crowood Press) accept no liability for any accidents, howsoever caused, to any reader following instructions from the text of the book.

Typefaces used: text and headings, ITC Giovanni; chapter headings, ITC Tiepolo.

Typeset and designed by
D & N Publishing
Membury Business Park, Lambourn Woodlands
Hungerford, Berkshire.

Printed and bound by Craft Print Pte. Ltd, Singapore

Contents

Acknowledgements

I am indebted to the many potters around the world who have generously given of their time and knowledge in enabling me to collect the information for this book, and I am especially grateful to those artists and photographers for providing, and giving permission to reproduce, their work.

My thanks are also due to Victor Harris of the British Museum and Rupert Faulkner of the Victoria and Albert Museum for setting me straight on many of my misapprehensions concerning Raku and the Japanese tradition.

My thanks are due to my friends, and especially to Rod Dorling and John Bell for bullying me into creating a far better book than I could have conceived and to Caroline Whyman for some necessarily harsh editing.

My thanks are also due to the Research Committee at the University of Wolverhampton without whose support this venture would not have happened, and to my colleagues and students whose inspiration made this work possible.

Introduction

'Raku' is a most evocative word. In the minds of contemporary potters and collectors it conjures up an alchemical brew of bins of smouldering sawdust: a pall of acrid vapour hangs over the kiln yard, and figures wearing huge gauntlets extract clay, in the grip of iron tongs, red hot from the kiln and plunge it into rusting buckets, pouring smoke. Later, pots emerge from these containers looking as if they have just been dug up from centuries of burial, oils and tars seemingly etched deep into their surface. Yet, after savage scarifying with wire wool, a glaze glistens on the work.

Other names of techniques and materials have a little of that exoticism – for instance porcelain, neriage, kaolin, celadon – but few have reached into the consciousness as has 'Raku'. It is a word of Japanese derivation which has been taken

Raku kiln firing. (Photograph by Rod Dorling.)

Raku kiln firing. (Photographs by Rod Dorling.)

over and embellished with more than fifty years of American and European Raku, until now we have something which is apparently quite different; yet the essence of that traditional Japanese meaning for 'Raku' is not merely just below the surface, but in fact provides a structure that informs much of current practice. In this book I wish to show the truth of this.

The foundations of Raku lie in a philosophical attitude to clay. Clay can take any shape: it is a truly mimetic substance. It shares a symbiotic relationship with a cultural past, feeding on the ceramic forms created throughout history. Clay itself is silent – it is the task of the potter to give expression to his or her own thoughts and

desires through the medium, providing a voice for it. Clay comes with a grammar, but not a vocabulary: that is, there are 'given' physical properties inherent in the material – for instance, according to whether the clay is gritty or smooth then certain forms and surfaces are easier to accomplish than others.

When we pick up something made in clay we also pick up a feeling for the history of its use, because pots are the materialization of human actions and embody a sense of the past. In their reinterpretation and idealization as icons, vessels create a material memory of life and experiences, and may serve to contain the viewer's thoughts and imaginings.

1 A Historical Overview

'Ichi-go ichi-e '… ('Each meeting only once')

The way that Raku came into our consciousness is, I believe, an integral part of a time when values were challenged and new ways of being in the world were examined. To an extent it summed up a generation's hopes that it might be possible to think through practice, a way of suggesting that there might be more than one right answer, and that direct, logical thought might not be the only way to reach these answers.

The Influence of Zen

Almost twenty years were to pass from when I first read about Raku to when I stood for the first time on Japanese soil – by which time I had been working in the Raku medium for almost as long. Back in 1973 I was still at university, studying (Western) philosophy. Its attitude to knowledge is one of critical evaluation, and its methodology a process of logical dissection: through breaking down structures and arguments in an analytical search for clarity and distinction we pursued 'Truth' and 'The Good' across the centuries. But in our time away from these studies we read of the exploits of training the mind of a Zen monk, and were regaled with stories from our friends who had returned from India, searching for enlightenment. In the same way as Western philosophy, Zen – this Japanese form of Buddhism – also asked about the meaning of life – of how to live a good life – but it followed a quite different agenda. It looked inward rather than outward, and instead of sharpening the tools of language in order to be able to ask the question in precise terms, and developing an acuity of mind required for the study of symbolic logic, Zen philosophy revealed a world of nuance and 'No-mind'. The aggressive interrogation of concepts was to be replaced with a meditative and receptive consciousness – even though the meditating monk was kept attentive through the long nights by blows from a cane wielded by his teacher!

The Central Significance of Tea

Yet another aid to staying awake was tea, containing the stimulant caffeine. Since its discovery and introduction from China a thousand years ago, tea has been revered in Japan. To contemporary Westerners it may seem extraordinary that this rather ordinary daily beverage has been imbued with mystic value by the Japanese, to the extent that they have a very significant ceremony surrounding its ritual drinking. But we need only consider the way in which tea and coffee were first received in our cultures to see that, of all commodities, they were once the most highly prized. If you read the Raku books you would be forgiven for thinking that all tea drinking is a religious experience: of course it is not, and as any tourist in Japan will tell you, it is as difficult to find this particular attitude to tea as it is to find Beefeaters in England. Some might see tea in the 'tea ceremony' (*Cha no yu*) as fulfilling a role similar to that of wine in the Catholic faith; but in fact to the Zen Buddhist it is about living in the 'here and now' – of discovering significance in just drinking tea – as opposed to looking outside our existence to another reality, as the Catholics believe, in the transubstantiation of wine. And it might be

worthy of mention here, that to Americans, the 'Boston Tea Party' carries yet another symbolic attitude to tea – a focussed response that sees it just as the commodity it is, and something that one can tip into the harbour if it serves a purpose, particularly that of freedom.

There is a world of ritual regarding tea that informs all the early history of Raku, and it provides the arena from which the name is derived. Standing at such a remove from that Japanese culture, as we do, it is hard not to put a romantic gloss on the tea ceremony – it is so very exotic, and quite outside our own experience. Consider that the first designer of Raku wares – which were made specifically for the consumption of tea – and the first great tea master, Sen no Rikyu, was told to commit ceremonial suicide: so he went back to his home town, put his worldly affairs in order, and did as his master had commanded. It is hard not to be fascinated by this kind of cinematic discipline.

Bernard Leach

The story of 'doing Raku' comes down to us in main part from the writings of Bernard Leach. In the first primer for craft potters, *A Potter's Book*, he describes his very first introduction into the world of firing: attending an epiphanic Raku firing in a friend's house – perhaps just as we do today. He and a group of other artists were invited to paint the pots provided, and then they were fired so that within the hour he had the glazed bowl in his hand. He writes ecstatically of this experience, and then says: 'a dormant impulse must have been awakened, for I began at once to search for a teacher, and shortly afterwards found one in Ogata Kenzan.' This is the enthusiasm that grabs the true Raku aficionado! A single year later Leach inherited a bundle of glaze recipes and the title 'Kenzan VII' from his teacher, Kenzan VI – and so he entered this mythological space in the Raku narrative.

In 1909 Leach arrived for the first time in Japan. It was a propitious time. He had been born in the Far East, the son of colonial parents; he had attended public school in England, and then,

*S*even images of the tea ceremony. (*Photographs by David Jones, with thanks to the Urasenke Foundation of Great Britain.*)

quite out of character for one of his class, decided he wanted to go to art school. After studying at the Slade School of Art for two years he decided to return to the East, to Japan, in order to teach etching. He fell in with a group of aesthetes and artists, chief amongst whom was Soetsu Yanagi, the main documenter of the resurgent folk-craft movement. Yanagi was well connected socially, and eased Leach's entrance into Japanese cultural life.

The Value of Hand Crafts

For much of the preceding four hundred years Japan had developed as a completely isolated island culture. The rulers had shut off practically all direct contact with the West, and as a result Japan had escaped the ravages of industrialization. (In England, by contrast, factory production and lower costs had all but obliterated the indigenous hand-made craft pottery industry.) There were two main legacies from this: the first was that the ceramics traded from Japan to England were actually a form of export goods, produced solely for the foreign markets, feeding the Romantic notion of the exoticism of the Far East. The second was that local Japanese potteries were still operating as they had done in the Middle Ages. For a man educated in the notion of a lost Utopia – taught to believe in the moral value of hand-craft production as preached by Ruskin and William Morris – Bernard Leach had arrived in a kind of earthly paradise. Japan was not merely a land where industrialism had not fully destroyed craft industries, but the products of those craft workshops were actually accorded the highest status by a discerning public: in Japan, craftsmen could earn a living!

Raku Tradition and the Tea Ceremony

The part of this cultural heritage that particularly interests us is the Raku tradition and the way that it has been influenced by the 'tea ceremony'. I want to use an analogy that I find useful because it draws a time-line for me and makes it relevant in terms of the history of my own country. Readers can find an analogy of their own that accords this otherwise strange story relevance.

In political terms the tea ceremony (*Cha-no-yu* in Japanese) held a place of significance in the lives of the Japanese analogous to that which in late Tudor England was occupied by the new Protestantism. The rulers used it as a means of advancement and consolidation of power, but it also had a very significant spiritual dimension. One of the main qualities of teaism is an untranslatable Japanese word: *wabi*, meaning the absolute antithesis of courtly opulence (it does indeed have something in common with Puritanism). But there is no reward structure in the Zen code: where the Protestant earns his right to a place in Heaven, the follower of Zen must accept that there is only this life. The attenuated feelings associated with *wabi* – 'withered ice', 'solitary and sad', 'poor and shabby' – help to attune us to acceptance of this fact. *Wabi* forces us to focus on transience: thus the simple act of taking a bowl of tea is a unique event, an occasion that will never be quite the same again.

In the seventeenth century this pureness inherent in the making and drinking of a cup of tea was elevated to the status of an 'aesthetic cult'; this came at the end of an historical period of developing spiritual thought and reflection, focusing particularly on removal from the world. In 'thinking of Zen Buddhism the mind abides nowhere – no-mind, that is, a mind should not possess a fixed abode which results in stiffness and obduracy' (*Raku* XV p. 58). A consequence of this belief led educated men to leave their rich palaces and comfortable homes and dwell in the forest or by a wintry lake, living in a poor hut away from the world, concentrating on just *being*. These are the qualities that are incorporated into tea ceremony: it is a sense of doing something that is in a special time, when the participants are quite away from the world. This place, this poor hovel, was then aestheticized and moved from the arid lake shore to a secluded spot at the bottom of a formal Japanese garden. It was to be used by the powerful to escape the demands of the day-to-day affairs of life, so they could focus on the here and now.

Tea Ceremony and Ceramic Expression

Towards the end of the sixteenth century in Japan there came a period of stability (like the end of the

Civil War in England, or the Thirty Years War in mainland Europe) when the country was unified under one ruler: Nobunaga. After his assassination further rebellions were quelled by a man who, like Henry VIII, was not merely war-like but also of great cultivated sensibility. Just as Henry encouraged court musicians and even wrote music himself, so the shogun, Hideyoshi, encouraged various forms of tea ceremony. Instrumental to this was his acquisition of the finest tea ware, and these pieces even went into battle with him, protected in their multiple boxes! To begin with there was a flamboyant display of excess – he had a tea ceremony organized at Kitano shrine for hundreds, if not thousands, of people, and its ostentatious proceedings were to have lasted for a week. (There is a parallel here with the 'Field of the Cloth of Gold', where the flower of English nobility went to France to exhibit the splendour of their possessions.) The tea utensils that were shown off were essentially of Chinese provenance. Sen no Rikyu was the Zen monk/tea-master who masterminded the development of these tea extravaganzas. He was a very significant figure in this tale because he also moved the tea ceremony in the counter-direction – towards an impoverished, *wabi* style that encouraged the use of a peasant-like ceramic, fashioned in a certain indigenous Japanese style. The ceramics used in this style were named after one of the characters in the name of Hideyoshi's palace: Jurakudai. The ideogram means enjoyment or pleasure: it is Raku.

This new form of ceramic expression ideally suited the aspirations of the samurai (warrior) class. Like the medieval knights in Europe, they were brought up to believe in a code of absolute loyalty and service to their lord, epitomized by total self-control and chivalry.

Chojiro

At the palace of his overlord, Hideyoshi, Rikyu commissioned a potter – always described as 'a tilemaker' – named Chojiro, to hand-carve bowls for the drinking of tea; but if one has ever seen a Japanese roof tile it will be evident from the skill involved that the tile maker was a sculptor and modeller of some considerable skill. According to some authorities Rikyu's greatest contribution to the tea and Raku aesthetic was connoisseurship. He designed many of the pots that Chojiro made, he collected some of the finest tea implements, and provided the rationale for developing this

wabi style. Such was the influence of Rikyu and the work of Chojiro that the latter was given the honorific word Raku to use as a family name. Hence Raku pots are those made by the family of, or more loosely in the style of, Chojiro.

Kichizaemon (Raku XV) is the direct descendant of this remarkable potter, Chojiro, and is regarded as one of the leading artists/craftsmen of his generation. In addition his exposition and understanding of the tea ceremony is very learned and scholarly, and is one of the texts on which I have based this resumé. Of course for him it is also a family *curriculum vitae* – a very significant difference to our personal experiences in the West where we probably have no antecedents who were potters in the craft tradition.

The Meaning of Wabi

There have been numerous attempts to define *wabi*, and it is important to understand its meaning as it determines so much of the development of Raku. That offered by D.T. Suzuki is: 'to be poor, that is, not to be dependent on things worldly – wealth, power and reputation – and yet to feel inwardly the presence of something of the highest value, above time and social position …' (in *Cha no yu* published by the Japan Society). It is in its contrast with the luxury that the noblemen were leaving behind that we get our best view of this austerity. Tea drinking came from the court of the Emperor of China, and to begin with there was a cult amongst the Japanese aristocracy for all things Chinese, from paintings to porcelain. There was a lavishness and grandeur associated with the expression of tea. Competitions would be held, in the manner of wine tastings, to identify different growths, and these events would be accompanied by gambling and exuberant entertainments.

The Celebration of Restraint

Once the military and their advisers took over teaism, an aura of sobriety was brought to the proceedings. By the end of the sixteenth century, behaviour of a ceremonially precise nature was required in all forms of social interaction. The

*S*eto tea caddy
with set of bags
and containers.
*(Reproduced by
courtesy of the trustees
of the British
Museum.)*

*B*lack high-fired
Ichinya tea bowl (left).
*(Reproduced by
courtesy of the trustees
of the British
Museum.)*

event would take place in a 'tea hut' that was based on a peasant dwelling. By contrast with the lavish affair held for hundreds of guests and designed for demonstrations of wealth and excess, the tea ceremony was now an event where the host would abase himself and actually serve his two to four guests himself! Instead of showing off the hundreds of objects in a collection, only a few choice objects were selected for that particular taking of tea. Originally these were the most advanced ceramics in the world: the bowls of the historic Sung dynasty, and contemporary Ming and Ch'ing porcelain.

By contrast with these highly sophisticated pots, exhibiting the most advanced technology of both clay and firing, Rikyu would create a collection of tea vessels for a specific occasion. These objects could be very diverse, and were a very original way of creating a 'set'. The ceramics could be historic artefacts, but more and more he came to depend on contemporary production. The mannered nature of poverty required an aged and lived-in appearance, and this led to the curious ceramic technique of quenching the red-hot pot in water to develop the accelerated crazing of the glaze (which also resulted in the frequent cracking of the clay), thus creating signifiers for age.

This is a practice that many potters have read about and then adopted in their own work (often in a fairly unthinking way). Many students have shown me broken pots and asked how to prevent this breakage, and the response of 'Don't drop a hot pot into cold water' is often met with incredulity. Potters can tend to adopt a technique lock, stock and barrel without looking at it critically. The important place that tradition has in our world should not preclude our examining what we have learnt, and omitting any part of the activity if it does not accord with our own aesthetic. Japanese Raku potters could get away with this because their aesthetic esteemed certain Raku pots so highly that a repair (with gold) could actually make the piece even more valuable.

The Ritual of the Tea Ceremony

In this way Rikyu laid the seeds for a distinctly Japanese practice, one in which the personality of the artist (as designer, potter, collector and tea host) could be encouraged to shine through.

Although the Samurai would leave their swords at the entrance to the tea hut where the ceremony took place, they did not leave their education and sensibilities. Connoisseurship was, and is, of great importance. There are prescribed rules for the handling of utensils and for the preparation of tea. It is a ritual of service and self-abnegation, where everything is done thinking of the guest as the absolute centre of attention. The actions of the host must have the natural familiarity of a practised ballerina – to us he appears to be making steps that are reminiscent of everyday actions, while also being far removed from them. This is a level of artifice that is very considered: it is an aesthetic withdrawal from the world, focussing on the ritual enacted in the restricted confines of the tea-hut, and on that alone. It is an unusual practice by men of power, for in history one is accustomed to seeing a move toward self-indulgence; however, it is possible that the discipline of the medieval Japanese warrior was similar to that of the early Shakers in America.

In most books on Raku this historical perspective is given merely as context. However, while this discussion may appear to be esoteric and have no relevance to our lives and ceramic experience today, I suggest the contrary: namely, I think that there are three main aspects of tea ceremony that can be teased out, given a modern gloss, and seen to be very informative about the practice of contemporary Raku.

The first is the centred attitude of mind encouraged by meditation: this can be seen to be essential at the point of firing and when the red-hot pot is removed from the kiln, when complete attention and focus is required to avoid either damage to the work or burning the artist! I would also presume to suggest that this openness and awareness is an ideal state of mind in which to approach objects – and in our case to be with Raku pots, and attune the mind in order to appreciate them.

Secondly, there is built in to this history of the beginnings of tea ceremony a play of opposites, namely the contrast between the luxury exhibited in the traditional Chinese artefacts and the apparent poverty of the first Japanese Raku items. We can also look at this contrast to illuminate the polarity between any custom and our own culture: thus a study of the old tradition tells us something about contemporary practice; it tells us how things have changed, although it is not a sense of progress – we surely do not presume to say that objects made now are better than the first tea-bowls. In this play of opposites is also embedded a classic paradigm of clay art – namely the contrast of court and country; rich/poor; luxury/austerity; smooth/rough; porcelain/low temperature clay; sophisticated/crude.

Thirdly, we can be informed about the nature of connoisseurship from this way of making a collection from apparently disparate items, to create a (quite ephemeral) set. We learn about the way in which art objects influence each other and set up a correspondence that is *more* than the sum of the different objects that make up a collection.

Raku: Tradition and Iconoclasm

When a form, pattern, decorative surface or glaze is recognized as being 'traditional', then that shape or surface brings with it a history: it represents not merely itself but all its predecessors, too. There is a certain appropriation of cultural

Tea bowl 'Window', Raku-fired, Dennis Farrell.

Tea bowl, Raku-fired, Camille Virot (see also page 107).

Two 'cup shapes',
Joy Bosworth.

Vessel, Verity
Eastwood. (Photograph
by Dave Jones.)

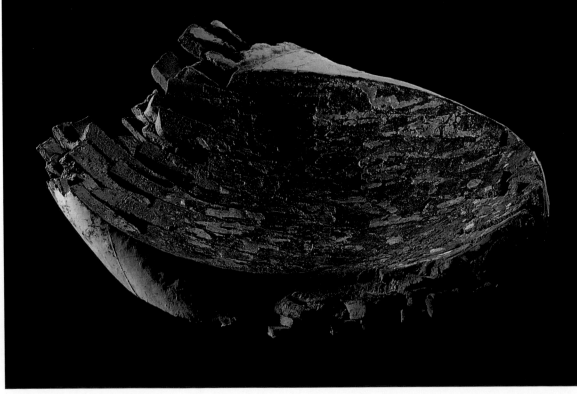

identity – and so we are led to think also of all the precursors of that pot (if we recognize them). Therefore by making work which looks towards, say, tea-ceremony ware, we set up a resonance in the viewer which adds to his or her delight in the experience, by reminding him/her of the historic pieces and the associated tea-ceremony activities.

It is also possible to put a negative gloss on the weight that tradition brings to bear on the shoulders of artists. It seems quite clear that Raku practice, amongst most other pottery expression in Japan, ossified in the seventeenth century and arrived in the twentieth century largely unchanged. Like many biological systems it had no need to evolve because it was ideally suited to its environment. Indeed this is still the case in Japan where Raku bowls are made and collected avidly: there is simply no reason to change that winning formula.

Herbert Sanders, one of the leading commentators on tea ceremony, writes of a crackle glaze: 'Crazed glaze is a requirement for Raku ware. A tea-master who is partial to its use

The Interior of Basho's tea-room. (Photograph by David Jones.)

*V*iew from the
tea house, Kyoto
(above).

*B*amboo fence, Kyoto.
(Photographs by David
Jones.)

*K*aiseki sweet, made
of sweet bean paste.
(Photograph by David
Jones.)

would tell you that bowls with uncrazed glaze disturb the aesthetic and calm atmosphere of the tea-room through the harsh, loud sound of the tea-whisk as the tea is beaten in the bowl.' (*The World of Japanese Ceramics, 1967.* Kodansha, p. 94).

Raku in the Twentieth Century

At the beginning of the twentieth century when Bernard Leach went to Japan as a young man there was still an attitude of mind in the West that regarded (and desired) things Japanese (and Chinese) as truly exotic and alien. As a result an acquisitive fascination for 'The Oriental' had developed, and, in response to this potential trade, the Japanese fashioned items specifically for the export market, blatantly exploiting that desire for the foreign.

When Leach returned to settle in St Ives he brought with him a vocabulary of authentic Japanese artefacts and processes. The objects used in the tea ceremony, with their exaggerated overtones of poverty and restraint, carried a quite different message to the over-decorated trade

wares so beloved of our Victorian forebears, and it was the former that influenced the next generation of potters in a most profound way. Leach certainly carried a Romantic notion of the untainted peasant, whose lineage stretched back to a golden past when everyone had their place in the social order; this was clearly a form of solace to an Edwardian gentleman. Leach's version of 'art and craft philosophy' and Eastern mysticism gained ground in post-World War II Europe and America; by the 1970s everybody needed a brown mug and a mantra. It was at this time that Raku really came into vogue – for instance, the drips on a Jackson Pollock painting could be equated with those on a tea bowl. Ceramics started to become mainstream and to claim a valid place in contemporary expression, and this mirrored the intellectual move from craftsmanship to creativity, from skill to art, and from repetition to originality.

Raku and the Americans

At this watershed Raku was re-invented by the Americans. Their attitude to clay, and particularly to Raku, was of 'suck it and see' – there was little reverence for the notion promulgated by Leach of the artist-potter as the only possible

*T*eabowl.
Kichiyaemon Raku XV.

'*A* fold within',
David Jones.
*(Photograph by Rod
Dorling.)*

saviour of the crafts, if not the whole human race. Untrammelled by either the class or the caste system, they relentlessly pursued an artistic notion of expression, and the purpose of the pot/vessel became not function, but to carry a personal message imparted by the maker.

Paul Soldner, working in California, was the natural inheritor of the 'New Frontier' code of the early American settlers. He read the account of Raku that Leach had written in *A Potter's Book*, of his quasi-religious induction into the inner sanctum of the Japanese craft world. Bernard Leach had demonstrated Raku in St Ives, in the inter-war years, to encourage an interest in pottery; this was as a stepping stone to the appreciation of the qualities inherent in the Chinese porcelains and stonewares. Soldner tried the technique that he had read about and, out of dissatisfaction with what had been achieved, embellished it: so after

taking the pot from the kiln, he rolled it in pepper leaves in the sidewalk – and obviously this dramatically increased the arena for artistic accident. It enabled the artist to experiment with aleatoric techniques that were becoming significant in the worlds of music and painting – that is, creating through a series of planned uncertainties: and this is the basis of almost all present-day Raku.

Present-Day Raku

The interpretation of that message is no longer the province of the potter-philosopher like Leach: it became the job of the audience, or critic. It was not a statement about truth to materials, nor about the sincerity of the potter: with

Raked stone Zen Garden, Kyoto. (Photograph by David Jones.)

*B*uildings in Kobe (right).

*P*alanquin at the Gion festival, Kyoto. *(Photographs by David Jones.)*

so much training removed from the workshop and installed in art schools, the emphasis lay more and more on visual truths rather than the hybrid East-meets-West philosophy of Leach and his friend Yanagi. The anti-machine ethic so beloved by the reactionary camp in the ceramic world went out of the window as space-race materials were pressed into service for kiln linings, and glass-fuming technologies for post-reduction treatments.

The colour range of traditional Japanese Raku is quite different to contemporary expression, yet there are superficial similarities. For instance, there is a preponderance of black in both palettes, the Japanese version of this being known as 'Black Seto' after the area of that name; to achieve the black coloration the potters created a glaze from a mixture of a stone from the local river in Kyoto, and lead ore. Western Raku is black due to carbonization from the secondary reduction. Western Raku and the Japanese Red Raku ware are both porous. This gives poor thermal conductivity, ideal for holding tea; it also gives a strange quality to Western Raku because the objects often feel lighter than one expects, as the clay is not fused. Curiously neither Japanese nor Western Raku glazes are very well balanced from a chemist's point of view; the decorative appearance and tactile qualities are considered to be more important.

2 Materials

One of the great attractions of *secondary reduction* is that it can involve no more than just throwing a red-hot pot into sawdust. The effects are not absolutely quantifiable or predictable, and although one can say with confidence that the effects will lie within certain parameters, it is impossible to anticipate precisely what the surface quality will be. It is the control and freedom in allowing things to happen that makes the process so seductive to both maker and collector: the potter is shaman negotiating with the kiln and orchestrating the marks left by secondary reduction. The feeling of 'birthing' the pot seems more vivid in Raku than in any other firing technique. Familiarity with the glaze tells us that the general range of qualities that can be produced is more varied than with other earthenware or high-fired surfaces; thus one can find oxidation, reduction, extreme reduction, reoxidation, and physical marking of the glaze by the reduction material occurring in very close proximity on a single glaze on a single pot.

Why Raku? The Motivation Behind the Practice

There is already quite enough published information on glazes, surfaces and decorative techniques to keep a Raku potter busy for his or her own lifetime and a little beyond. Hasn't all the testing been done? Haven't all the questions been asked? Behind us stretch three hundred and fifty years of Japanese tradition and fifty years of American and European practice: is the

future to be just imitation and derivative ideas? I shall argue that it is not. The first questions for the practitioner are:

'Why am I doing Raku?'
'What is it that I hope to find by firing my work, processing my ideas, in this way?'
'What do I hope to discover?'
'What precise effects do I require?'
'Can I cope with cooling cracks in my work?'

These are questions that it is good to ask before the event, but can sometimes only be answered after *'Doing'*.

Ways of Using Materials

It is possible to consider all the materials and techniques used in this process, and then to devise some new uses of materials. Some of these developments require careful planning and forethought; others just need us to be with the process and they will arrive. Novel ways of manipulating a fixed range of materials and methodologies can happen with no real conscious effort, just through working. This is Zen teaching in practice: don't make too much deliberate effort to evolve something new, and through 'Doing' a new understanding of the possible will come. If this sounds too optimistic, then I must temper it with the suggestion that we stop periodically and reflect on the practice that has evolved; in this way we arrive at a new goal that is born of a marriage of thought and action.

What, then, is the starting point? There are two general principles that guide research into ingredients and ways of using them. The first principle is that we know nothing; thus, starting from simple materials and processes, without prejudice, we discover ways of using anything that comes to hand – our own thinking is moved forwards by this openness of thought, and is not restricted by the past. The second principle refuses to reinvent the wheel. It examines the body of knowledge built up over time, and is discovered by looking at tradition, books, seminars and master classes – it is a cumulative set of experiences that exists to be built on. We can steal someone else's invention and use it to our own *original* ends.

The first point of call on our journey is the simple *empirical*: what happens when we heat material 'X' in a kiln, or when we mix these two apparently immiscible materials? The second is the empirical/*theoretical* area which asks 'why?' and which provides an explanation of what we observe in terms of more general principles. This is chemistry. It is a system of explanation that describes what happens in many different applications. Many artists do not find scientific explication easy to comprehend, and baulk at any of the ways of discussing the world in abstract and symbolic language. My years of teaching chemistry-phobic students has tempered any natural enthusiasm for this type of explanation, so most of the accounts of glaze and fired surface in this book will not require a detailed understanding of chemistry except when it is actually easier to remember because abstract symbolic language acts as a shortcut.

OBSERVE AND DOCUMENT

Regardless of theory, the most important aspect to bear in mind when using this book is to **observe as closely as you can and to document results accurately.** After all, no potters before the nineteenth century had the benefit of this full scientific language, or a complete understanding of the Periodic Table. The great ceramics of the past – tea-ceremony ware, Chinese porcelain, English slip-ware and so on – were all achieved with a more primitive sort of explanation, with scant knowledge of atoms and valence! In contemporary Raku glazing we often use a set of very refined and carefully constructed chemicals as our starting point. If one looks at a recipe in any of the Raku books it tends to be an account in terms of frits; this is a group of sophisticated, manufactured, non-toxic and insoluble materials. However, this is not where Raku began, nor where I think it is leading – but they are materials that I use every day. I shall look briefly at an account of that historical world

of Japanese ceramic as related by Bernard Leach, and trace it through to other low-fire technologies. What is interesting about Japanese Raku and saggar firing is that both are operating with very simple and primitive glaze-firing materials and technologies. It is contemporary Raku practice to incorporate these products of twentieth-century science into our practice.

In most situations what we find is that the more sophisticated a material, the simpler and more perfect is the quality of glaze surface. This is the goal that frits were first designed to reach, satisfying the needs of industry for stable, safe materials. Used in a conventional firing this can result in a perfect, but bland, surface. In Raku, these materials result in very simple recipes and an ease in achieving a better quality of glaze surface. I believe that Raku is about complexity and richness of fired surface (although often executed on a form of great simplicity and perfection). These heterogeneous attributes are conferred in post-firing reduction, and the associated techniques of pit and saggar firing push investigations on into further areas of primitive complexity. These developments will be examined in more depth in Chapter 3.

The Chemist's Explanation

This section will hopefully give a more profound understanding of what is going on. (As potters we only have to take what is of use to ourselves and we can revisit it later.)

Periodic Table

This apparently daunting diagram is a very concise way of showing family resemblances and relationships between elements. For example, the first column shows the alkali metals lithium, potassium and sodium which all behave in similar ways in order to melt, or flux, the glaze. The encoding system for materials started in the time when Latin was the language commonly spoken by scientists, as well as the one used to discuss artistic and religious ideas. It was the new philosophy of the natural world, so it is not surprising that some of the chemical symbols still in use

Table of Elements Useful for Raku

ELEMENT	CHEMICAL SYMBOL (AND LATIN NAME)	FOUND IN THE FOLLOWING CERAMIC MATERIALS	EXAMPLE OF COMMON SOURCES
Hydrogen	H	Clay	Water (H_2O)
Lithium	Li	Lithium carbonate	
Carbon	C	Carbonates	Carbon dioxide (CO_2) (in the atmosphere)
Oxygen	O	Oxides	Water
Sodium	Na (natrium)	Soda feldspar, high alkaline frit	Salt (NaCl)
Aluminium	Al	Clay	Saucepans
Silicon	Si	Flint/silica; clay, frits	Glass, sand
Potassium	K (kalium)	Potash feldspar, high alkaline frit	Plant fertilizer
Calcium	Ca	Calcium borate frit	Chalk/whiting
Lead	Pb (plumbum)	Lead bisilicate	Roof gutters
Manganese	Mn	Manganese oxide	Steel alloys
Iron	Fe (ferrum)	Ferric oxide	Rust
Cobalt	Co	Cobalt oxide	Steel
Copper	Cu	Copper carbonate	Electrical wiring, roofs
Tin	Sn (stannum)	Tin oxide	Coating on iron cans

today are in this ancient language; for instance the symbol for lead is Pb from *plumbum*. There are only a few elements and their symbols that we need to remember, and these are enumerated in the illustration.

Defining Elements

An element is pure in the sense that it does not contain any material other than itself. If you take a look at any pottery workshop it will doubtless be so mucky that you would never believe that anything pure would be found there – and you would be right, because except for a gold wedding ring, an aluminium bottle top or iron nails we shall find no elements in this strict sense of the word. Most relevant to our purposes would be the oxygen contained in the atmosphere: this is an element so reactive that nearly all other elements combine with it, and thereby produce oxides. In ceramics we are greatly interested in oxides (and carbonates), because when they are heated they do not produce any unpleasant by-products. They have the added advantage for glaze composition in that they are fairly insoluble. To appreciate the relationship between them and its relevance to, say, colour in glazes, it is important to understand how an element is made up; thus:

An *atom* is the smallest part of an element that can take part in a chemical reaction. But some elements, such as oxygen, can only exist as *molecules*. Moreover, although the atoms of any one element are all exactly alike in every respect, they are different from the atoms of every other element.

A molecule is the product of that combination of two or more atoms; the product of two different elements is called a *compound*.

What we see when we isolate a grain of a ceramic material is a *particle* of a compound that is composed of thousands of molecules, which are too small to distinguish.

Periodic Table of Elements Useful for Raku

KEY

Atomic Number	21
Name	Nitrogen
Symbol	N
Atomic Weight (H=1.008, O=16)	14.008
Number of electrons in outer layer	5

Numbers given to the families or groups

Metals

Fluxes

Group 1	Group 2
3 Lithium Li 6.940 1	4 Beryllium Be 9.02 2
11 Sodium Na 22.997 1	12 Magnesium Mg 24.32 2
19 Potassium K 39.096 1	20 Calcium Ca 40.08 2
	38 Strontium Sr 87.63 2
	56 Barium Ba 137.36 2

Chief Ceramic Colourants / Metals with slightly irregular characteristics

3a	4a	5a	6a	7a	8	9	10	1b	2b
21 Scandium Sc 45.10 2	22 Titanium Ti 47.10 2	23 Vanadium V 50.95 2	24 Chromium Cr 52.01 1	25 Manganese Mn 54.93 2	26 Iron Fe 55.85 2	27 Cobalt Co 58.94 2	28 Nickel Ni 58.69 2	29 Copper Cu 63.57 1	30 Zinc Zn 65.38 2
	40 Zirconium Zr 91.22 2							47 Silver Ag 107.880 1	48 Cadmium Cd 112.41 2
							78 Platinum Pt 195.23 1	79 Gold Au 197.2 1	

Non-Metals

Glass-Forming Oxides

3	4	5	6	7	0 (Inert Gases)
				1 Hydrogen H 1.0080 1	2 Helium He 4.003 1
5 Boron B 10.82 3	6 Carbon C 12.010 4	7 Nitrogen N 14.008 5	8 Oxygen O 16.000 6	9 Fluorine F 19.00 7	10 Neon Ne 20.183 8
13 Aluminium Al 26.97 3	14 Silicon Si 28.06 4	15 Phosphorus P 30.98 5	16 Sulphur S 32.076 6	17 Chlorine Cl 35.457 7	18 Argon A 39.944 8
31 Gallium Ga 69.72 3	32 Germanium Ge 72.60 4	33 Arsenic As 74.91 5			
	50 Tin Sn 118.70 4	51 Antimony Sb 121.76 5			
	82 Lead Pb 207.21 4	83 Bismuth Bi 209.00 5			

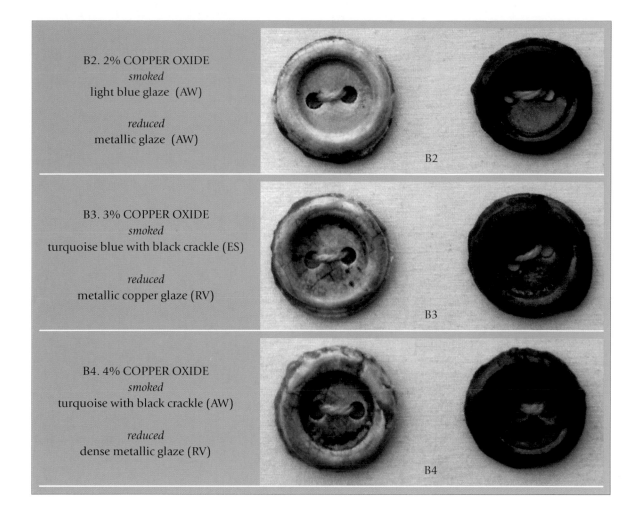

B2. 2% COPPER OXIDE
smoked
light blue glaze (AW)

reduced
metallic glaze (AW)

B2

B3. 3% COPPER OXIDE
smoked
turquoise blue with black crackle (ES)

reduced
metallic copper glaze (RV)

B3

B4. 4% COPPER OXIDE
smoked
turquoise with black crackle (AW)

reduced
dense metallic glaze (RV)

B4

An atom is composed of a positively charged nucleus surrounded by negatively charged electrons. In a compound, metal atoms give up electrons to non-metal atoms, and the number of electrons that can be relinquished in this way determines the combining power (or *valency*) of the atom; for example, copper can give up either one or two electrons. CuO is the common state for copper salts in our atmosphere in the presence of sufficient oxygen; when one copper atom reacts with one oxygen atom it gives the fully oxidized form of copper, leading to green and blue glazes. The figure above shows the oxidized and reduction colours of copper (Ros Ingram).

Controlling Colour

In a normal reduction-firing the oxygen in the kiln atmosphere is depleted so that only half as much reacts with the copper; then two atoms of copper react with each atom of oxygen to give Cu_2O, this gives rise to red colours in a glaze. We can control the colour of a glaze by controlling the kiln atmosphere surrounding the molten, still reactive glaze. In Raku we have two opportunities to achieve this: the first is in the kiln and is known as 'reduction', when the amount of air (containing oxygen) entering the burners is partially restricted once the glaze has melted. In Raku the glaze is still molten when the vessel is removed from the kiln, and this is the opportunity for 'secondary' or 'post-firing' reduction.

This latter process, more than any other, has come to define contemporary Raku practice: the pot taken red hot from the kiln and placed with its glaze still molten into sawdust. On contact the nearest sawdust is rapidly heated, and is desperate to combust; but to do so it requires oxygen, and since the pot is smothered by further layers of sawdust, it must take the oxygen it would need from the oxides in the glaze: thus the green copper glaze turns to reds, or more likely to metallic copper, as the electrons are stripped from the atom. After cooling, the 'reds'

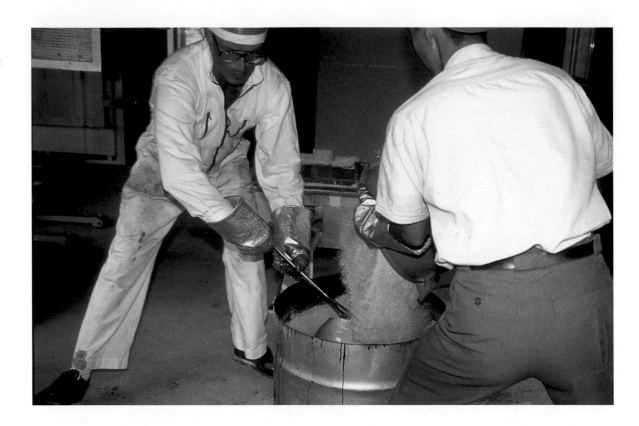

(from Cu$_2$O) and 'copper' (from Cu) are only loosely bound to the glaze matrix and can slowly re-oxidize in the atmosphere. Thus we have the phenomenon of the metamorphosing glaze that can turn from harsh new penny colour to soft turquoises, unless they are sealed with lacquer! This phenomenon can also be recognized in the way that a copper roof will change to green in time.

The Ingredients in Glazes

Frits

An analysis of most low-temperature Raku glazes shows them to be closely allied to glass (a glass being a 'super-cooled liquid'), the chief difference between them being that the glaze is more viscous. In practice a glaze generally contains increasing quantities of clay as the temperature of firing is increased; thus at porcelain firing temperatures the glaze and body are of a very similar nature. (In compounding Raku glazes from glassy frits I have found it to be beneficial to include a nominal 10–15 per cent of clay to help stabilize the colours and glaze surface; it is also an aid in the liquid glaze to keep it in suspension.)

The main constituent of glaze and glass is the compound silica (SiO$_2$); this will melt by itself to form a glass at the phenomenally high temperature of 1713°C – it might be added that at this temperature most of our *kilns* would melt! Early technology in both pottery and glass production in the Near East discovered a fundamental rule of chemistry: that a mixture of two materials will always have a melting point lower than the melting point of the most refractory (meaning 'resistant to high temperatures') of the two ingredients. (Later scientists have given the name 'eutectic' to the point of lowest temperature where melting occurs: this gives an ideal composition for a glaze.) It was discovered that mixing sand with either of two materials found in the area made a material that would melt at high bonfire temperatures: these two locally occurring compounds were lead ores, extracted from the rock, and alkalis which could be found on the surface of the desert. Lead is highly toxic, and free alkalis are very soluble. As our glazes are normally waterborne we need to incorporate these materials into suspension in an insoluble and non-poisonous form. This is done through making a frit.

Frits are one of those many 'anonymous' white powders that are sold by pottery suppliers to be added to glazes. Many have very mysterious codenames such as Ferro 3110, or Pemco 658; however, these are just a means of classification, and the analyses tell us what the actual working chemicals are. To make frits the constituents are heated together in a crucible until they have melted, the melting point of the mixture being determined by the proportion and nature of the ingredients mixed with silica. These added substances, that encourage the glaze to melt at a lower temperature, are known as fluxes.

Fluxes

The flux materials employed in glazes are metal oxides: they make the glass/glaze flow by interfering with the crystal lattice arrangement of the silica molecule, thus making it less stable and lowering its melting point. Potters generally use the metals found in the first two columns of the periodic table as these give a clear base glaze; they also use lead and boron compounds.

Each metal oxide flux will give a subtly different colour with sensitive reagents, such as copper, ranging from green with lead, through to turquoise and blue in alkaline and borax glazes.

To make a frit, the molten liquid is poured into water where the liquid compound freezes into droplets. These are then ground and dried and sold to us in packets. Different fluxing agents are active at different temperatures.

Glaze test. Eggs, Ros Ingram.

Fluxing Agents		
OXIDE	TEMPERATURE AT WHICH FLUXING ACTION BEGINS (°C)	QUALITIES CONFERRED BY FLUXING OXIDE IN RAKU GLAZES
Lead	500	A softer texture
Borax	700	Lack of elasticity – boron oxide will reduce crazing in small quantities, and then encourage it as its proportion increases (borax is a slight anomaly in that it is a low melting-point material that acts both as a flux and also as a glass-former)
Potassium	750	Sugary. High contraction, leading to crazing
Sodium	800	Sugary and crazes extensively
Lithium	800	More runny. Inhibits crazing
Calcium	1100	Matting

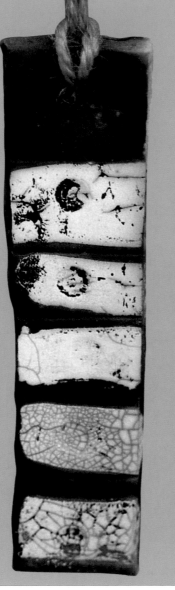

Test Tile of Five Frits,
Ros Ingram

(1) LEAD BISILICATE
Bisque: clear glaze, slightly crazed under surface.
Raku: white glaze with a few crazed lines.

2) LEAD SESQUILICATE
Bisque: clear glaze, with yellow tinge.
Raku: white glaze with a fine crackle.

(3) CALCIUM BORATE FRIT
Bisque: white, slightly crazed glaze.
Raku: white glaze with a very fine crackle.

(4) HIGH ALKALINE FRIT
Bisque: pinkish clear glaze.
Raku: white Raku glaze with a large amount of crackle.

(5) SOFT BORAX FRIT
Bisque: white glaze with a fine craze under the surface.
Raku: white glaze with a crackle.

Revision of a Historic Glaze

These frits are the materials used in the most recent history of Raku. When Raku was first documented in the West by Leach, Hal Riegger and others, the materials listed in their recipes were quite different. Leach's classic recipe was given to him by his Japanese teacher (Kenzan); it was the first recipe that doubtless many other potters and I used for our first glazing – it is:

White lead	66
Quartz	30
China clay	4

This recipe contains simple materials. It adopts the normal ceramic convention for a glaze recipe: the proportions of the glaze add up to one hundred, the glaze is colourless (additions of colouring oxides are added on top of this 100%). Proper names are used: for instance, white lead = lead carbonate. Unfortunately this is a very toxic glaze; if this (slightly soluble) form of lead is ingested it will be stored in the human body, and the cumulative effects will lead to lead poisoning.

In 1978 Bernard Leach revised his text, substituting lead frit for the lead carbonate in this recipe. Lead frits are characterized by their chemical names which depend on the amount of silica bound to the lead oxide molecule, and using the Latin prefixes for 1, 2 and 1½. Hence we have lead monosilicate, where lead and silica are present in a compound in equal proportions; lead bisilicate, where the proportion is 1 lead oxide: 2 silica; and finally, lead sesquisilicate, which is halfway between the two. All forms can find their way into glaze recipes, depending on the maturing temperature of the glaze. A current (safe) version of a similar glaze would be:

Lead sesquisilicate	94	or 95	for better suspension of the lead in water
China clay	2		
Silica	4		

Leach also advocates the use of seaweed glues (siccatives) to help the glaze adhere to the pot. Leach was firing in the Japanese style using a

So how does one choose the correct frit from amongst the vast range for sale? When I was in Japan I was forced into this situation: I was given a range of different frits to try. This became interesting, because in England I only ever use one frit (because that works!). What was fascinating was that using different frits in my glaze recipes and firing at 750°C, 1000°C and 1150°C, didn't seem to make much difference to the quality of glaze surface – they were all very glassy; it was only discernible in the colours of the copper glaze, which were greener in the very low temperature frit – perhaps suggesting that there was more lead in the lower melting frit. This shows the need for observation and testing to give us the final information we need for our work.

very thick application of glaze. As most potters nowadays do not fire a glaze so thickly, these binders are to an extent redundant. Nowadays we would use gum tragacanth, gum Arabic, or PVA to bind successive layers of glaze.

Methodologies of Testing

'I love the way that you just can't tell what effect you are going to get with Raku!'; and, 'Raku glazes are just so unpredictable.' These are the typical responses that many potters and I have given when we first do Raku. Perhaps, after a time, this excitement palls; certainly there comes a time when most potters want to direct and orchestrate the range of effects at their disposal, and so a need for rigorous testing arises. Firstly, though, one must experience Raku, and other methods of firing ceramics at low temperatures, and enjoy the apparently random marks and accidental qualities burnt into the clay. These effects can be very elusive, until the same procedure is repeated a large number of times. After this considerable acquaintance with a given process we can still not give an absolute description of a given surface, but we can identify the parameters within which a glaze will fire, or the kind of markings possible – that is, we can identify the rough ball-park within which the surface will be found. Experience and testing are the ways that we can make these predictions more assured, and the potter more able to speak with confidence of the results.

At the beginning of this chapter I started a discussion of the different ways of acquiring knowledge in a scientific manner; however, theory can only get us so far, and the important aspect is the empirical – one must physically test the material(s), recipes, firing procedures and post-firing reduction techniques for oneself, in a kiln with which one can become familiar. It is also very useful to repeat the processes and to fully document the results, then draw conclusions of how the processes work in the particular instance of that kiln and those glazes, through a comparison of repeated results.

It is useful to get to grips with ceramic materials knowledge in a systematic and cumulative way, using all the available information supported by any prior knowledge. It is advisable to mix up a recipe from the latest magazine article or book, as well as to become acquainted with the nature of materials and processes in an isolated manner; in this way you get to know the single materials quite intimately, and then as part of a larger picture. One might look at this way of accumulating knowledge not so much as the reinvention of the wheel, but rather as looking at how different wheels are constructed; then one is equipped with sufficient knowledge to choose the best one for the task. With glazes it is always worth asking why we ought to use a sophisticated four-wheel-drive when a wheelbarrow will do!

Single Material Tests

The first piece of knowledge to be gleaned is that of the nature of the individual materials in isolation, in given firing conditions. After that it is possible to construct scenarios for examining the substances in combination. There are three criteria for selecting these materials for testing: firstly, from prior knowledge; then from research into books; and finally one can use divine inspiration! There are many selections made *for* us – for instance in the ceramic materials catalogues, the school or college glaze room, the shelves of a pottery – but it is essential that nothing stops us from **adding** to this repertoire: this might be specific ceramic materials taken from other areas of clay, or they might be additions from outside the glaze room such as acrylic paints or local crushed rocks.

Isolate the materials to be tested, then apply them to a slab of clay with depressions pressed in to prevent any of the materials sliding off the clay when they are molten. Determine a method for assessing when to stop firing, and if required, when to remove the tests from the kiln.

When conducting these experiments it is helpful to use the sophisticated methods of temperature testing – a pyrometer or pyrometric cones – until one can assess when a firing is completed just by looking at the molten surface of the glaze in the kiln. After identifying the range of materials to be used, one should test the materials in combination.

DESIGNING A TEST TILE

The first task is to design a test tile. This should be representative of the work to be fired, and should provide as much information as possible – ideally it might even provide answers to questions that were not considered, such as colouring half the test with a different coloured slip, and coating the clay with a series of thicknesses of glaze.

The test-tile design should reflect the current style of work, have vertical and horizontal areas on which a glaze might run and pool, a stripe of another coloured slip, an area of texture, and a means of attachment to a board and for collection afterwards – a hole that can take a nail or string? If you are planning to experiment with secondary reduction then you will also need a means of removing the test from the kiln (the hole again?), plus features to ensure its stability when standing within the kiln. Application of the test material should have at least three different grades of thickness of glaze applied – thick, normal and thin; but one may want to experiment with very thick double dipping in the style of the Japanese Raku masters, or thin wiped-off washes like milk.

Particularly in the testing of Raku surfaces it is worth making half a dozen of each tile because there is so much variety and latitude of possible effect, as the temperature of firing and of secondary reduction can vary so much. A possible range of tests after removal from the kiln might be:

1. left to cool in the air – oxidized;
2. left to cool a little until the glaze has frozen, and then reduced;
3. transferred immediately to a reduction bin containing, in turn, sawdust;
4. straw;
5. wood shavings;
6. oil;
7. wet leaves;
8. grass;
9. grain;
10. sprayed with tin chloride and transferred immediately to a reduction bin containing, in turn, sawdust; etc.

Simple Testing Procedures for Ceramic Materials

LINE BLEND

After examining the results of the tests with isolated materials one can examine how they combine in a test called a 'line blend'. The procedure is to weigh the materials and to mix them into water. They are applied to the test tile by using the mode of application to be used in the work:

spray, pour, paint or dip the glazes. The tests of materials 'A' and 'B' are mixed according to the following code:

A	0	1	2	3	4	5	6	7	8	9	10
B	10	9	8	7	6	5	4	3	2	1	0

One needs eleven test tiles, or spaces on a strip of clay for the glaze tests. For example, mix number four will be a glaze composed of 30 per cent of material A and 70 per cent material B, and so on.

If the materials are mixed up wet as suggested and one uses 100g of material A and 100g of material B and each is mixed into equal volumes of water, then one can use volumetric measurement in order to get the quantities of material. Mix number four will be three spoons of A and seven spoons of B. It is much quicker to work by known volumes than to weigh each proportion individually.

For the foregoing experiment one might have chosen soda ash and china clay; this would give a clear glaze. Colour, or another material, can be added using the same methodology. One looks at the results and decides that, say, mix number three is the quality of surface that one wants to proceed with (20 per cent of A and 80 per cent of B). Then mix up a double volume of this glaze, divide it in half and place into two containers, and then add a colouring oxide to one of the mixes and call this mixture B and repeat the experiment. One can continue to modify this glaze by adding other colouring oxides or other materials. At each new starting point one knows exactly what is in mixture A and B, and what each test represents. These results should be written down and annotated.

A LINE BLEND OF COLOUR

For colour tests it is good to add double the recommended percentage of oxide (*see* page 34) – for example 5 per cent – to one mix of the base glaze (A) and make a line blend with the base glaze with no additions (B). Each of the intervals will represent decreasing concentrations of ½ per cent intervals.

The first space on the tile will represent 5 per cent; the second space will represent 4½ per cent; the third space will represent 4 per cent; and so on.

Labels on test strips: FRITS ON THEIR OWN · LEAD BISILICATE · LEAD SESQUILICATE · CALCIUM BORATE FRIT · HIGH ALKALINE FRIT · ...AX FRIT · LINE BLEND OF COPPER AND HIGH ALKALINE FRIT · RAKU

Ros Ingram line blends: plus test on frits.

Having performed this whole set of operations a few times, one then has a number of viable glazes that can be mixed, using this simple technique.

Another way to deal with the two glazes is to overlap them by pouring one over the other; spraying one, two or three layers over a dipped glaze; and so on.

Glaze

The composition of glazes is dependent on temperature. The higher the temperature, then, in principle, the greater the amount of clay, or other alumina and silica-rich materials that can be included in the glaze; this makes a glaze more viscous and helps to prevent it from running off the pot.

When a Raku pot is fired, the clay body does not go very hard – it is not vitrified, and the glaze is also soft; the significance of this is that if the fit between them is not good, or if the glaze is underfired, then it is all too easy for the glaze to flake off.

Colour

The expression of colour in a glaze is best understood through practical observation. Unless one has extensive glaze experience it is difficult to predict what any combination of materials will do, and even the experts are often surprised by the physical result. (Most potters who have fired another potter's well tried and tested recipe in their own kiln have often found that the results rarely come out as desired! Nonetheless this is a good place to start.)

Colour is the effect of binding various metal oxides into the matrix of silica, alumina and flux that constitutes the base glaze or frit. The metal oxides used as fluxes have no inherent colour, and for coloration we use what are known as transition metal oxides (so named because of their place in the middle of the periodic table, *see* page 26). Non-potters will be familiar with these as the metals used in everyday life: iron, copper, cobalt, tin, and so on. These transition metal oxides will produce a fairly consistent set of colours, although some, particularly copper, are strongly affected not merely by the presence of different flux materials but also by the atmospheric condition in the kiln and any post-firing reduction.

There follows below a list of the oxides, and the approximate percentages and colour range that we can hope to get from each. The convention used by potters writing glaze recipes is to give the clear glaze to 100 per cent, and to add the colouring oxides as an additional percentage at the bottom of the recipe.

Lustre

One of the important Japanese meanings of the word 'Raku' is 'enjoyment', and there does seem to be a sense of *joie de vivre* about most firing, even if we are closely focussed on a successful product. One of the earliest observations of Western Raku was that it encouraged the development of lustres. These are similar in appearance to the clay paste lustres as produced in the great ceramic traditions of Persia, Turkey and, later, North Africa and Spain, yet they are produced with a lot less anxiety and much less need for precision. On the other hand, the lustres are less permanent even than the clay paste ones, being far more susceptible to reaction – that is, re-oxidation and attack by sulphur pollution in city air.

Some of our earliest observations of lustre come from old glass dug up out of the ground: humic acid eats into the soft, reactive top layer, and in a matter of just a few years produces an aged, glinting patina, with the light refracting out of the pits etched into its surface. Damp sawdust can produce a similar effect on Raku-fired glazes, creating facets of glaze and giving the appearance of an object lost by a now-forgotten civilization. Where lustres and the semblance of gold was – and is – a quality surrounded by secrecy and repeated with great difficulty by lustre-ware potters, it is achieved with alarming ease in contemporary Raku. Multi-layering of glazes by spraying can encourage iridescence, by producing very thin translucent layers.

COPPER AS COLORANT AND LUSTRING AGENT

Copper is a ubiquitous ceramic colorant so it is not surprising to find it appearing in so many Raku glaze recipes, but it is hard to ensure that it does *not* lustre! To get a Mediterranean turquoise and not a new-penny bronze can sometimes be surprisingly difficult in secondary reduction. When a molten glaze containing copper oxide is immersed in sawdust, then all three colour states can exist (that is, two forms of oxide and pure metal in, or on, the alumino-silicate glaze

RECOMMENDED CONCENTRATIONS OF COLOURING OXIDES

Iron	brown, green and yellowish glazes: try 2–15%
Cobalt	blue: 1–5%
Copper	green, blue, turquoise, red, bronze: ½–20%
Manganese	browns and purples: try the difference between alkaline and lead-based glazes, 1–8%
Silver	yellows and gold lustre: 1–2%
Gold	purple, pink: ¼–1%
Tin	white: 5–10%

COLOURED GLAZE RECIPES

Basic glaze recipe:

High alkaline frit	85
China clay	10
Bentonite	5

OXIDE ADDITIONS

Blue
Cobalt oxide	2

Turquoise
Copper carbonate	1

White
Tin oxide	7

Purple of Cassius
Gold chloride	¼

Silver/gold/yellow
High alkaline frit	50
Lithium carbonate	35
China clay	10
Bentonite	5
Silver nitrate	1.5

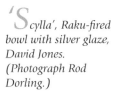

'Scylla', Raku-fired bowl with silver glaze, David Jones. (Photograph Rod Dorling.)

'The Dreyfuss study' (6ft × 6ft/2m × 2m), copper and silver Raku-fired lustres, Susan and Steven Kemenyffy.

matrix). If reduction is arrested at this point then we have a glaze that can have different layers and thicknesses of oxides sitting on its surface. These reflect, refract and absorb light slightly differently. These different waves of light coming from the surface have a similar wavelength and these interfere, intensifying some colours and cancelling out others, to create an effect like oil on water.

Smoking

Smoking is a term that refers to a lighter reduction than direct contact with reduction materials, and is achieved by standing the pot on a bed of sawdust and covering it with an inverted bin. It is the ideal technique for the rainbow-coloured development of the copper matt glaze. This is a glaze of finely divided copper bound by a little frit.

Recipe	
Copper carbonate	90
Frit	10
Bentonite	5

*L*ine blends of copper oxide and china clay, Pip Gittings.

If you look into the kiln as this is firing, then you can see that the green carbonate very quickly breaks down to the black oxide. The pot is removed and placed on a pile of combustible material; smoke is produced, which is trapped by means of an inverted bin around the still hot and reactive glaze. If the reduction is interrupted by lifting the container, then oxidation occurs and very thin films of oxide are unevenly deposited on each other, and iridescence occurs, due to thin layer interference. This is a spectacular glaze, which can be very seductive.

Smoking is also the favoured technique of post-firing reduction for the development of the resist slip surface (*see* page 51) and is also the best technique for staining white crackle glazes with smoke to make the lines go black.

FUMING

Fuming can encourage these iridescent colours. In this process a very thin layer of material is deposited on the glaze surface; for instance tin chloride solution can be sprayed onto the surface of the red-hot glaze as the pot is being removed from the kiln, or it can be sprayed into the kiln itself as a volatilizing vapour, as some salt glazers

Button Tests (Ash White, Earth Stone and Red St Valentines), *Ros Ingram*

SMOKED   REDUCED

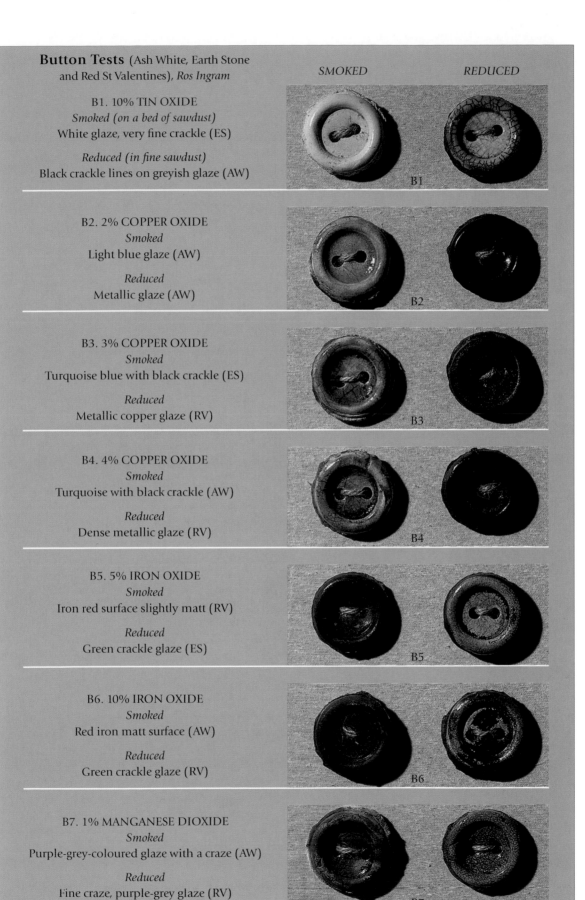

B1. 10% TIN OXIDE
Smoked (on a bed of sawdust)
White glaze, very fine crackle (ES)

Reduced (in fine sawdust)
Black crackle lines on greyish glaze (AW)

B2. 2% COPPER OXIDE
Smoked
Light blue glaze (AW)

Reduced
Metallic glaze (AW)

B3. 3% COPPER OXIDE
Smoked
Turquoise blue with black crackle (ES)

Reduced
Metallic copper glaze (RV)

B4. 4% COPPER OXIDE
Smoked
Turquoise with black crackle (AW)

Reduced
Dense metallic glaze (RV)

B5. 5% IRON OXIDE
Smoked
Iron red surface slightly matt (RV)

Reduced
Green crackle glaze (ES)

B6. 10% IRON OXIDE
Smoked
Red iron matt surface (AW)

Reduced
Green crackle glaze (RV)

B7. 1% MANGANESE DIOXIDE
Smoked
Purple-grey-coloured glaze with a craze (AW)

Reduced
Fine craze, purple-grey glaze (RV)

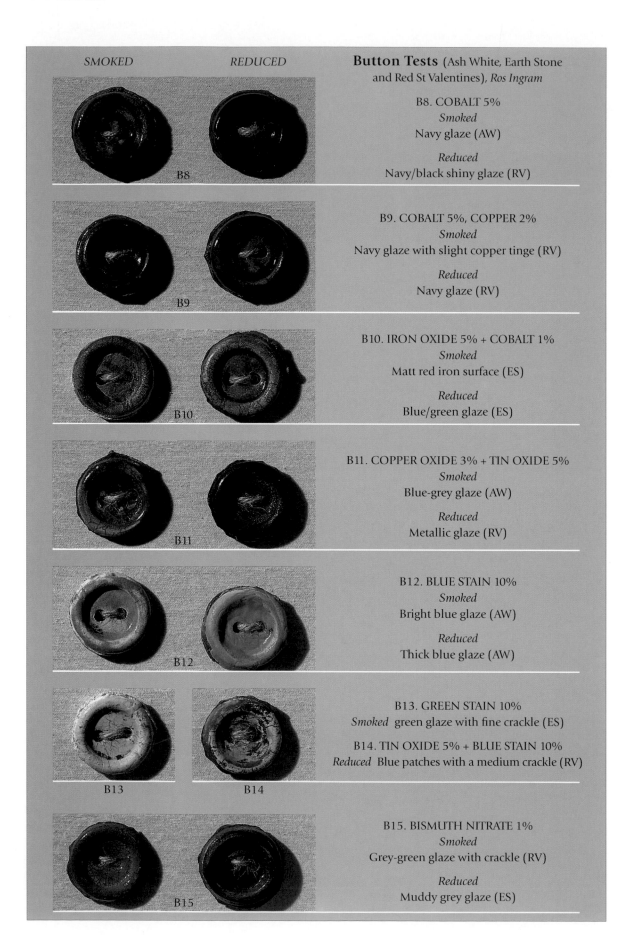

SMOKED   REDUCED

Button Tests (Ash White, Earth Stone
and Red St Valentines), *Ros Ingram*

B8. COBALT 5%
Smoked
Navy glaze (AW)

Reduced
Navy/black shiny glaze (RV)

B9. COBALT 5%, COPPER 2%
Smoked
Navy glaze with slight copper tinge (RV)

Reduced
Navy glaze (RV)

B10. IRON OXIDE 5% + COBALT 1%
Smoked
Matt red iron surface (ES)

Reduced
Blue/green glaze (ES)

B11. COPPER OXIDE 3% + TIN OXIDE 5%
Smoked
Blue-grey glaze (AW)

Reduced
Metallic glaze (RV)

B12. BLUE STAIN 10%
Smoked
Bright blue glaze (AW)

Reduced
Thick blue glaze (AW)

B13. GREEN STAIN 10%
Smoked green glaze with fine crackle (ES)

B14. TIN OXIDE 5% + BLUE STAIN 10%
Reduced Blue patches with a medium crackle (RV)

B15. BISMUTH NITRATE 1%
Smoked
Grey-green glaze with crackle (RV)

Reduced
Muddy grey glaze (ES)

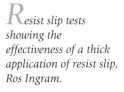

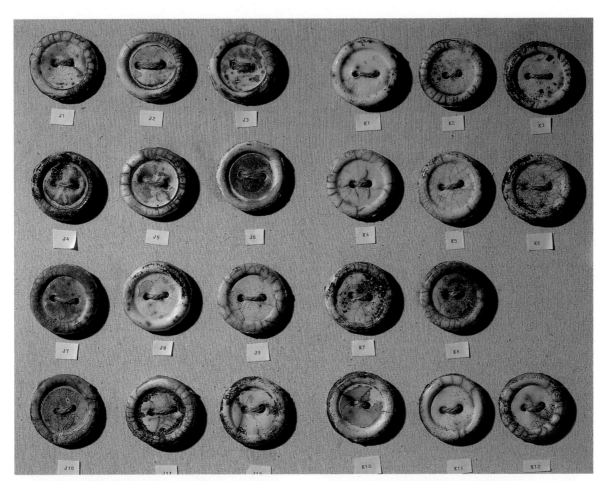

Resist slip tests showing the effectiveness of a thick application of resist slip, Ros Ingram.

'Raku vessel', fumed copper and acrylics, Rick Foris (far left).

Removing a pot from a red-hot kiln, John Wheeldon.

*S*prinkling sawdust on red-hot pots, John Wheeldon. This should be carried out using protective clothing.

*F*uming copper matt-glazed pots, under tins, John Wheeldon.

*P*ots exposed briefly to the air to allow re-oxidation, to develop a fumed copper glaze, John Wheeldon.

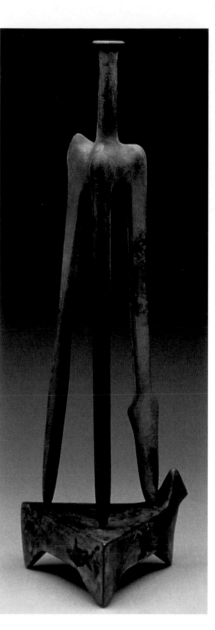

'Three monks' –
*fumed copper matt
glaze (26in (67cm)
high), Irene Poulton
(far left).*

*'Primal bowl with
weapon artefact #3'
– fumed copper in
sigillata slip, Rick
Hirsch.*

do, and the entire kiln fumed. (Tin and chlorine are toxic, so proper respiratory protection must be worn – be sure that you have a proper filter on your mask.) Silver nitrate, or indeed photo waste containing silver, can be used in the same way.

SILVER/GOLD LUSTRE

A lustre using silver can be like a mirror. Silver nitrate dissolves very easily in tap water and precipitates out as a yellow solid; this quickly oxidizes to a black colour. In the glaze it can vary from shiny gloss to a matt, reticulated metal with all the variants in between, as the degrees of reduction increase; this is dictated by the type of reduction material employed, dense fine sawdust creating the heaviest reduction and straw one of the lightest. If the glaze is still molten when it strikes the reduction material then the latter's texture – say, straw – can also be picked up. There is a similarity here with a glass blower's technique, but whereas he has minutes to work on the hot surface, the Raku artist has but seconds to manipulate the effect.

In preparation for post-firing reduction everything must be carefully planned in advance: reduction zones must be carefully cleared, and any sprays of water or fuming agents placed to hand. Safety is paramount. Speed and precision of movement must be co-ordinated. The piece can be left to air-cool a little to encourage the

Health and Safety

Wear skin and eye protection when handling silver nitrate as it is corrosive.

Two Raku vessels with a stripe of gold glaze created by silver nitrate, David Jones. (Photograph by Rod Dorling.)

cracking of the glaze known as 'crazing', or it can be moved to a reduction chamber as quickly as possible to gain the maximum effect from the reduction. A crackle glaze pot that is deposited swiftly into sawdust can actually absorb carbon into the glaze, and this can give shades of grey and brown as well as an iridescence.

THE EFFECTS OF TIME ON LUSTRE

The lustring imparted by silver nitrate can be somewhat short-lived, the bright mirror-like surface of the silver glaze moderating to mother-of-pearl over a period of years, in much the same way that the old paste lustres become gentler over time. This happens as the silver metal, which is not tightly bound into the glaze matrix, reacts with the common gases in our atmosphere (oxygen and polluting sulphides). The slow reactions of these gases with silver give rise to the tarnish on cutlery. The consequence of this is that the colour of the pot modifies, with time, towards a much subtler and more autumnal feel: the tea masters would have called this 'more *Wabi*' (this is certainly how one would describe the changes in copper glazes). It is possible to make the lustre more permanent by effecting an in-kiln reduction; this will give a lustred quality throughout the depth of the glaze rather than just at the surface. To do this, cut off the air supply to the still-combusting gas entering the kiln so that the hot gas takes the oxygen that it needs to burn from the oxides in the glaze instead. Subsequently the glaze can be sealed with silicone polish, which delays oxygen penetration of the glaze.

Clay

Raku pots are removed from the kiln and allowed to cool rapidly; this process leads to *thermal shock* that is perceived as cracking (*see* p. 45). History tells us that (Japanese) Raku pots are made from coarse, gritty clays, to give maximum thermal shock resistance; thus Raku books are filled with recipes for lumpy clay bodies with a high level of porosity and absorption. Current experiments, however, have devised clay bodies

Raku-fired 'Wing form', Mike Marshall.

Saggar-fired, interlocking slip-cast forms, Louise Shepherd.

that confer the same level of thermal shock protection but have a finer texture (they are often much more expensive). A clay body is a manufactured mixture of fine and coarse clays, sand and other fillers that give particular qualities for different ceramic applications.

Another alternative is to use the clay body that one is presently using and observe how it performs – then you can assess whether the loss rate is too great. If it is, then another clay must be substituted, or modifications made to the existing clay body. It is not really possible to substitute a slip-casting clay, though you can minimize the problems of cracking with protected cooling.

Clay and Heat

Cracking in ceramic results from too rapid a heat change for that thickness of clay. Raku has traditionally been characterized by a process involving rapid heating and sudden cooling effected by quenching in water. This causes stress, because as the clay cools it shrinks: if the clay is thick, then the outside layers will quickly become much cooler than the core which will have retained the heat, and a tension develops between the particles on the outside contracting much more than those in the centre of the wall. From this we can deduce that the clay that allows slight movement of particles against one another is going to survive

'Mounted raku form with mended decorative cracks.'

Peter Hayes has tackled the problem with thermal shock cracks, and turned it on its head by making a virtue of the cracked and glued object, actually rejecting clays that '… don't crack enough'. He fills cracked and broken areas with coloured resins, which echoes the way that some of the earliest Japanese tea bowls were repaired, using gold in the cracks. He jokes that the mends are stronger than the pots!

better than one which has a glassy continuity. The disposition to crack is there in all clays. It starts at the surface, and the particles pull apart as the clay starts to cool and shrinks. If the material is even (fine clay particles) and continuous (semi-vitrified) then the crack will start and develop, eventually splitting at an edge. If the clay is discontinuous – that is, composed of particles of differing sizes – then as a crack develops it will be unable to progress, its development being literally prevented by a large lump of low-expansion material in its path. The ideal clay body is one composed of particles of irregular size, and which does not vitrify at the temperatures at which we are working (that is, does not become glassy).

The phenomenon of thermal shock requires a little explanation in terms of the physics of clay. Clay can be considered as a complex molecule composed of alternating layers of silica and alumina, separated by chemically combined water. These platelets are separated by fillers like sand (silica), grog and physically combined water; this latter is a replaceable form of water and enables the clay to be dried and reconstituted any number of times at room temperature. However, once the chemically combined water is driven off in the bisque firing then it is no longer possible to return the material to plastic clay: it has become ceramic.

THERMAL SHOCK

At 227°C and 560°C the 'free (crystalline) silica' molecules undergo a twist when they are being heated – they increase in size by up to 3 per cent; correspondingly, when they are cooled they shrink by the same amount (ceramic chemists refer to this twisting expansion in the clay as the alpha/beta quartz inversion). This is where the real potential for cracking occurs, because if the clay section is thick, then the outside layers will suddenly jolt apart as the clay shrinks, but the hotter interior does not shift until it has reached this critical temperature – and the tensions involved will cause a crack to penetrate throughout the clay wall. There do happen to be clays dug straight out of the ground that have almost the ideal composition to prevent this happening: the fireclays associated with coal seams.

CLAY BODY COMPOSITION

Fireclays are not ideal for use in their raw form, although they are relatively inexpensive. They were created by sedimentary deposition in prehistoric seas and are often associated with lime deposits (chalk) left by unicellular organisms. This can lead to what is known as 'lime spit-out' after the bisque firing: the chalk is dehydrated in the firing and then rehydrates in the air, and it expands, pushing off a piece of pot and leaving an unsightly hole. To prevent this phenomenon it is probably worthwhile to get a filter-pressed

clay body: the production method of such a clay involves frequent washing during its manufacture, and this removes the lime.

Formulation of a Raku Clay Body

The best starting point is a clay with some of the following characteristics:

1. **Low flux content**: Some clays – even white ones – will melt at Raku temperatures because they contain impurities leading to vitrification. Such clays should be used with care.
2. **Plasticity**: This is conferred by particle size: the smaller the particles, then the more water is associated with the greater surface area and the easier it is for the molecules to slide over one another. The best materials are *ball clays* and *Bentonite* (a very fine volcanic clay-like material).
3. **Low expansion materials**: This will comprise *grog* (pre-fired clay that has been ground finely enough not to interfere with our building techniques), *molochite* (a ground-up, white, pre-fired clay), *talc* (chemically magnesium silicate), a very low expansion material, and *kyanite* (a micaceous material).
4. **Coarse materials**: These are the best fillers to prevent cracking – although a consequence of adding too much can lead to the composition of a very gritty and rough body that is 'short' (that is, having very low plasticity). Even the finest groggy materials will be millions of times bigger than the largest clay particles (for example *sand*, *grog* and *molochite*).
5. **Fine smooth fillers**: In practice, most potters who throw tend to choose clay bodies with smoother and finer particles, as these will be kinder on the hands – for instance, *fine molochite*.
6. **The correct colour for the work**: A white clay will provide a ground for intense colour development. Iron-bearing clays will impart a warm, muted quality.

Health and Safety

If one is mixing clay bodies from dry material it is important to observe Health and Safety precautions: that is, to minimize dust in the atmosphere and to avoid inhaling it.

TYPICAL SAMPLE CLAY RECIPES

These coarse clays have the benefit of a low water content, so there is not a high level of shrinkage associated with their drying.

1. Any stoneware clay with an addition of grog and molochite.
2. A mixture of 'T' material and porcelain, approximately in the proportions of 1:1 to 2:1.
3. Fire clay 60, plastic stoneware clay 20, talc 10, grog 10.

MANUFACTURED CLAY BODIES

'T' Material: This is a widely used clay body, manufactured by Morganite Thermal in Cheshire, England; its recipe is secret. It was said to have been used for making refractories; however, it was actually developed as a hand-building clay, and this has been its use for decades because it has a very low shrinkage on drying due to the high quantity of pre-fired material it contains. This also provides its thermal shock resistance. (Morganite's spokesman explained that the appellation 'T' derives from the fact that

it was first made and marketed by a firm called Cooper and Tidman in Treforest, Wales.)

'T' material is an ideal clay body for Raku. In analysis it is approximately 42 per cent alumina, the most refractory fraction of the clay formula, though unfortunately it is a little coarse and non-plastic; it is also brittle when it dries. (It may help to imagine such a clay as being composed of a high proportion of gritty particles with particles of clay between them, which act as a glue; however, there are insufficient small particles for it to form a strong structure.)

Porcelain: This is made from ball clays, plastic china clays and non-plastic, fluxing materials, with the addition of Bentonite. An advantage of mixing such a clay to a refractory clay such as 'T' material is that it improves green strength; also, with its propensity for melting, even at the relatively low temperature of Raku, some of these particles sinter and fuse together, making for a stronger body. Of course, this has to be tempered with the knowledge that this will predispose the clay to suffering thermal shock. A white clay like 'T' material/porcelain is ideal for the development of bright, clear colours, since most other clays contain a proportion of iron – the

*V*essel, *Raku-fired with resist slip decoration, David Roberts.*

oxides of iron will give a pinkish hue to bisque-fired ware and a muted effect on the glazes.

OTHER MANUFACTURED CLAYS

Kiln furniture was traditionally referred to as 'cranks', and the name has been coined to describe another type of clay body available from manufacturers: this one is based on (cheaper) red clay rather than the more refractory white clay that 'T' material uses as a basis. There can also be the problem with 'lime spit-out' because some of the filler in the clay is crushed fire-brick. Nevertheless, this clay has been very successful on the British market, and so of course there have been attempts made to create bodies with similar qualities. Chief amongst these is 'Y' material manufactured by Potclays, and the new 'Earthstone' range manufactured by Valentines.

Improving the Clay Surface

USING SLIPS

You may want to use a red or a very coarse clay for reasons of economy or for scale of building, in which case you may also then want to obliterate the iron colour and smooth out any pitting: to do this you can cover the clay surface with a white slip. A slip-painted surface also achieves very bright, pure colours, and provides a flat ground for painting on.

Slip Recipe	
China clay	85
Silica	15
Zirconium oxide	2

*D*econstructed teapot – detail showing texture of 'T' material. David Jones (above left). (Photograph by Rod Dorling.)

*S*eated figures, Sally Macdonell (above).

*'H*olding piece', sawdust fired, Antonia Salmon.

BURNISHING

A slip is one way to provide a smooth surface; it is also possible to compress the clay particles and even produce a mirror-like shine by polishing the surface with a pebble or the back of a spoon, a process known as burnishing. It is suggested that this works by aligning all the plate-like clay molecules in the same direction, so that they reflect the light.

Burnishing has been used since the earliest periods of pottery production to aid waterproofing, and has long been used as a decorative surface in its own right, the polished, shiny areas of clay contrasting with the rough, unpolished ones. It is also possible to burnish slip and thereby produce a surface that is both shiny *and* a different colour to the background. Burnish will be progressively destroyed as the temperature of firing rises and the clay sinters; however, this normally

occurs just above the normal firing range for Raku, so the two could be said to be ideally suited to each other. Applications of slip will also read through a glaze so one can start to establish a repertoire of surface composed of glazed, slipped, burnished and rough areas of clay.

CARBONIZATION

As contemporary Raku practice so often involves secondary reduction by plunging the red-hot pot into sawdust, thereby creating carbonization, it is worth observing the behaviour of slips and burnished clay in these conditions. The smothered red-hot pot is nestled in sawdust that contact has heated to red-heat. The sawdust carbonizes – like charcoal – because it is starved of oxygen. This carbon vapour (soot) is absorbed into the open spaces in the clay and

*S*triped black and white 'humbug', resist slip and smoked decoration (diameter 20in (51cm)), Tim Andrews. (Photograph by Sam Bailey.)

*T*est pieces fired to demonstrate the difference between Raku (right) and low-temperature saggar with salt and sawdust (left), Dennis Farrell.

Raku-fired vase-form decorated with sigillata *slip and resist-glazed, Roland Summer* (right).

the pot goes a lustrous black, where well burnished, or shades of grey where the smoking is less intense; white and pinks can occur where more oxygen is present and the reduction carbon is burnt away. Smoking will modify and even obliterate the colours of any applied slip that is not protected by a coat of glaze, which prevents carbonization.

Two tall bottles with resist slip decoration, David Roberts.

RESIST SLIPS

The observation that a glaze prevents soot impregnating the porous clay body has been

exploited by Dave Roberts, Tim Andrews and Roland Summer. These practitioners developed their technique having noticed that if the glaze fell off their ware, a craze pattern of smoke marks on the bare clay was revealed. (This might have happened, for instance, to pots left out in the garden which were soaked with rain and then victims of frost action: this would lead to spalling of the glaze, so that the clay body (protected) beneath was revealed.) The clay was still white, but where the smoke had penetrated a crazed, pitted or damaged glaze surface, the crack lines remained in the white clay as a tracery of black lines, or dots.

In order to ensure that the glaze came off the clay surface, potters originally tried to sandblast the glaze, mimicking the action of frost. The next stage is to apply a layer of high melting point (refractory) slip onto the bisque-fired clay – if the biscuit pot has been sealed with a *terra sigillata* slip and/or burnished, then resistance to sticking will be greater still. The resist slip must be carefully applied as it has a high raw clay content: it must stick well enough not to fall off before firing, but its adhesion must be weak enough so that it flakes off easily *after* the glaze firing. This slip is composed of materials that do not sinter and melt onto the clay: quartz (silica) and china clay (with a possible addition of alumina powder); zirconium oxide is another refractory material that can stop the slip becoming glassy and sticky.

During the firing the glaze melts; when the pot is removed from the kiln it is allowed to air-cool a little, because this encourages crazing, and then it is either completely buried in sawdust, or stood on top of it and covered with an old tin can. The latter method allows smoke penetration of the glaze; burying the pot completely makes the whole of the body under the glaze go grey. The slip 'fits' so badly that it flakes off, taking the glaze with it. The piece is washed and scrubbed to remove all further traces of slip, and after drying, the clay surface can be sealed with beeswax or silicone polish.

This is a quality of surface whose complexity is best suited to very simple form – plain vessels seem to be the ideal vehicle. Any roughness will provide a site where the slip can stick, and then protuberances are more likely to be broken off in cleaning. Here, therefore, form is subsidiary to the decorative surface. (*See* p. 39 for series of tests on thickness of resist slip, sigillata, and crackle development.)

Dave Roberts has further exploited this phenomenon by drawing through the glaze and slip and creating a set of fuzzy black lines. This pattern is revealed as the glaze peels away, although unlike the craze pattern in glaze which is glassy, this is an interplay of matt qualities or a very subtle shine produced on bare clay. Tim Andrews is developing a whole repertoire of decorative qualities based on soot lines over coloured slip bases: the pattern is the physical trace of the glaze that shrinks and crazes due to its very high level of contraction – as lines of weakness develop between large plates of glaze, then the soot can penetrate and stain the clay body. Tim also noticed that faults in the glaze surface created by bubbles led to black circular marks in the staining of the covered clay, and he has devised a low-tech glazing methodology to accentuate this feature. By blowing through a length of pipe into the glaze he creates a froth on the surface and imperfections in the glaze surface; these bubbles create holes in the glaze through which the smoke can penetrate and so

make a pattern of random dots in the burnished slip beneath!

TERRA SIGILLATA

One way to maximize the play of colour and combustion is to apply a levigated slip known as a *terra sigillata* slip. (The application of levigated slips to clay reached its zenith in the Roman era: this slip has taken for its name the Latin for

Vessel with pink slip and resist slip decoration, Tim Andrews. (Photograph by Sam Bailey.)

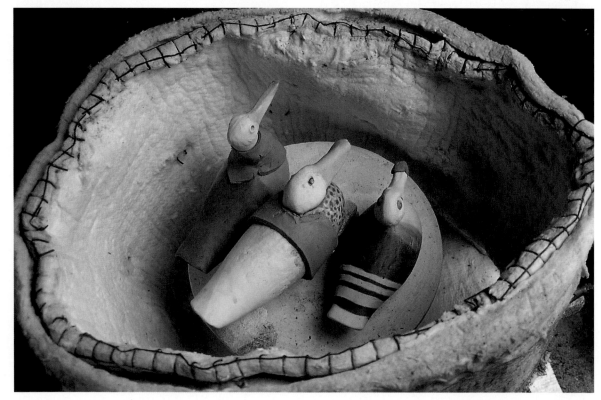

*T*hrown form: sawdust saggar-fired, Pam Salter.

'stamped clay', the way that most work was finished.) It is composed of the finest particles that make up a clay, and is prepared by slaking down a dry clay with distilled water and a deflocculent (wood ash lye sodium hexametaphosphate (calgon) or sodium silicate prevent the clay particles from sticking, or flocking, together); at first the clay forms a cloudy suspension in a bottle, then it starts to settle out. The last fraction to precipitate is composed of the finest particles, and this needs to be siphoned off from the solids that have collected, and saved; it should have the appearance of milk. I have mentioned already how sigillatas can be used under a resist slip to give a smoother surface. On pit-, sawdust- and saggar-fired pots it provides a shinier, more receptive canvas for marking, and the porous clay can then be sealed with a judicious application of beeswax or silicone polish; but you might decide not to use a polish as it can give a very shiny surface.

Terra Sigillata Recipe

0.5kg Clay
4g Water softener (sodium hexametaphosphate)
1.5 litres Distilled water

*K*iln *showing ducks decorated with* terra sigillata *and 'wearing' clay resist jackets to protect them from secondary reduction when they are removed from the kiln, Susan Halls.*

3 Firing

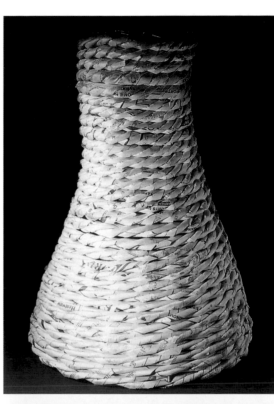

A *mould made from paper and copper wire fashioned to make a basket, Sebastian Blackie.*

Mythic History

To the earliest humans, our ancestors, fire was both a commodity of inestimable value and also a mystery demanding reverence. As hunter-gatherers they would travel from one food source to another on long migratory journeys, and in order to make much of what they ate digestible they would cook it in a fire; this increased the range of foodstuffs available for consumption, and on the whole enabled those peoples to adapt to an environment more successfully than animals which relied on their digestive systems alone for dealing with food. On their travels these humans would not merely have taken their minimal belongings, but they must also have actually transported fire itself (rubbing sticks together is a much more recent discovery). Fire would have offered protection from the animals over whose territories they ranged, and would thus have extended the distances over which they could travel safely. It could have been carried over short distances by placing burning embers in a leaf, or in a receptacle fashioned from woven leaves and twigs: a basket. Lining that basket with mud would protect the organic materials from which it was woven, and this meant that the travellers could range further. It was also observed that the clay-mud hardened as a result of being heated, and became a very useful container that could be sealed with plant juices and used for food storage. It has been suggested that the earliest pots derived from this observation.

Although many of the earliest ceramics that have survived date from millennia after these beginnings, historians point to the evidence that they have a basket motif as a pattern. There are modern manifestations of this fascination with fire and the palaeolithic past, such as Sebastian Blackie's basket-fired constructions.

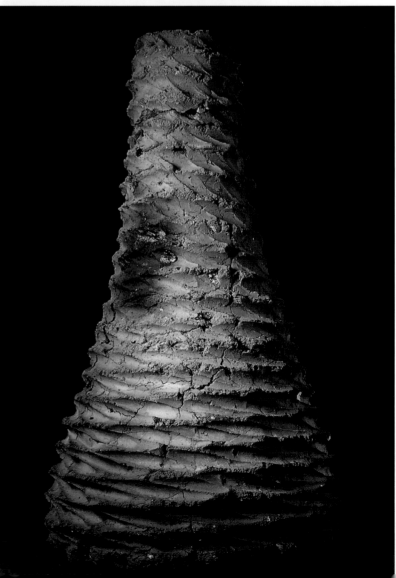

The finished object – the mould lined with clay and fired, Sebastian Blackie.

*T*rough, saggar fired, paper clay, Hazel Thomson.

measuring progress from the outside by means of pyrometric cones or pyrometers. The glaze, which has been applied as a powder, puckers and collects into globules; these gradually smooth out, and the glaze matures as the pin-holes close over. At the temperatures normally used in Raku we can treat the glaze very much as a glass and, indeed, many of the post-firing processes associated with Raku come from a glass-making methodology, for instance fuming. While the glass/glaze is liquid it is reactive – it is alive and available to the maker for surface treatment. If one is actually looking to mark the glaze with a post-firing – otherwise known as 'reduction' – treatment, then it is important that the glaze remains fluid for long enough. How successfully this is achieved depends on the speed with which the pot is removed from the kiln and the thermal mass of the piece (that is, the heavier the clay is, then the longer it takes to cool down – and the thicker the clay walls, then the more heat that is stored).

The Kiln and Its Transformative Power

At its most basic a kiln is a container for retaining and regulating heat. It works on the principle that for the temperature inside the kiln to increase, the amount of heat put into it must exceed the rate of heat loss. The most basic firing structure is a bon-fire, and indeed this reaches temperatures which are sufficient not merely to change clay to ceramic, at a dull red heat of approximately 600°C, but also to melt some Raku glazes at around 900°C.

The most basic kilns are formed by digging a hole in the ground, or surrounding the bonfire with turves of grass or shards of broken pottery in order to conserve and regulate the heat evenly.

The kiln is also an alchemical chamber in which powdery materials are transformed to lus-trous glazes. However, in order to achieve this magic one needs to understand not merely how to achieve certain results, but also why they happen.

Combustion

Heat for kilns comes from the oxidation (burning) of hydrocarbons (wood, gas, coal and coke), or electricity, which is derived from these materials or from renewable resources. Hydrocarbons are created by plants from water and atmospheric carbon dioxide, using energy from the sun, in the process called photosynthesis. Combustion is when those dried plant materials are burnt, in a reverse of that reaction, with atmospheric oxygen.

In conditions of plentiful oxygen the carbon atoms that have been chemically linked together produced, poisonous carbon monoxide and finely divided carbon are created. This reducing flame has a yellow colour due to the refraction of light from the carbon specks; it does not release as much energy as in full combustion, simply because it does not burn as hot. (Secondary reduction, the hallmark of Raku firing, is a hot process involving oxygen starvation which occurs outside the kiln.)

The air taken in at the point of ignition in a gas burner is known as the 'primary air'; that taken in later through gaps deliberately left in the kiln walls is called secondary air. One such

'Unsuspecting the siege', carbon-stained clay, Gail Bakutis.

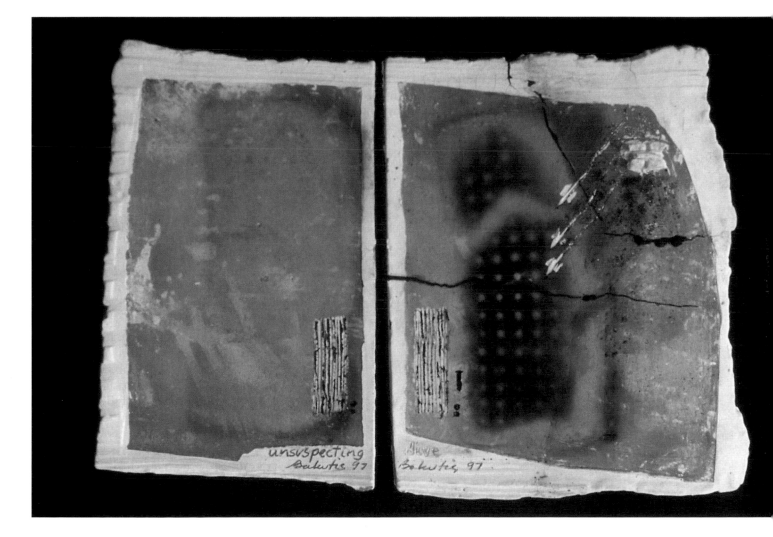

are broken apart releasing that energy – an oxidizing atmosphere. In the kiln this is characterized by a clear or blue flame colour, and all the carbon is burnt to carbon dioxide. If the oxygen supply is restricted, then not all the carbon can be oxidized, and this is called a reducing atmosphere. Also, instead of carbon dioxide gas being gap is generally left around the burner so that additional oxygen can be pulled into the kiln along with the pressurized gas.

When a bonfire is started the energy supplied to the wood by a match ignites the wood. Volatile hydrocarbons (wood gases) are produced. The energy supplied by the burning

*S*imple updraught wood-firing kiln:
brick firebox and clay chamber,
Steven Charnock.

A Refurbished Kiln for Raku

One can easily recycle old kilns and re-use the refractories and casing to give them a new lease of life as a Raku kiln. Most kilns are manufactured to withstand temperatures in excess of 1300°C, but at these temperatures the insulation needs to be superior, as any heat loss can be very costly. So once large cracks have appeared in the mortar and the door no longer fastens, and the kiln strains to reach temperature, it is time to recommission it for Raku. A gas kiln may require very little adaptation at all: it will have burner ports, so it can just be moved outside. With an electric kiln the metal elements must be removed and a hole for the burner(s) cut through the bricks and casing; however, this is easy with a drill and jigsaw. Always wear protective clothing, eye protection and dust mask.

Raku Kiln Made From a Recycled Gas Cooker

If you don't have access to old refractories in a kiln then you need to be more enterprising. This recycled gas cooker is a project devised and assembled by student Matt Strong at Wolverhampton University. He started from the premise that recycling was an important activity and that price had to be kept to a minimum. He

RCF-lined gas oven, Matt Strong (above).

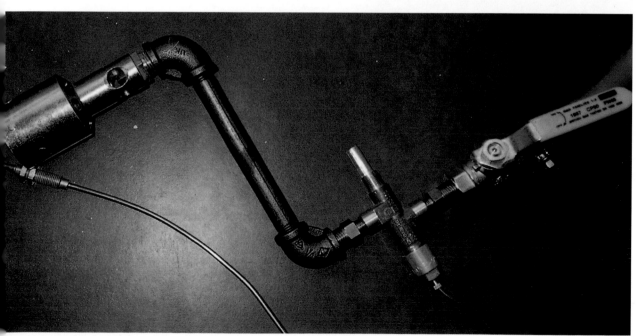

Burner set-up, Matt Strong.

theorized that 'an oven is designed to retain heat and would therefore have some insulating properties'; it is also of sturdy construction and would already have a door attached. He rethought its orientation, and used the flame access point at the base as a flue by exchanging the top and bottom panels; he cut a hole in the door for a spy hole, and in the back for the burner. The fibre was stuck on with refractory cement, thus avoiding the need to drill holes for ceramic buttons, and then sprayed with rigidizer. In order to even out the temperature from the single burner, the ware would be stood on a kiln shelf to allow circulation of heat below the pots.

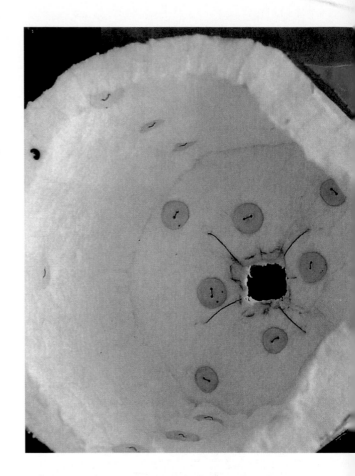

Simple Top-Hat Raku Kiln Assembled From Ceramic Fibre

Expanded metal makes an ideal backbone on which to hang insulation material; it is a relatively inexpensive form of framing that can be bought from a builder's merchant, and from which any size of structure can be made. Proceed as follows: bend the mesh into a cylinder and fasten it. Make the top by cutting into the top of

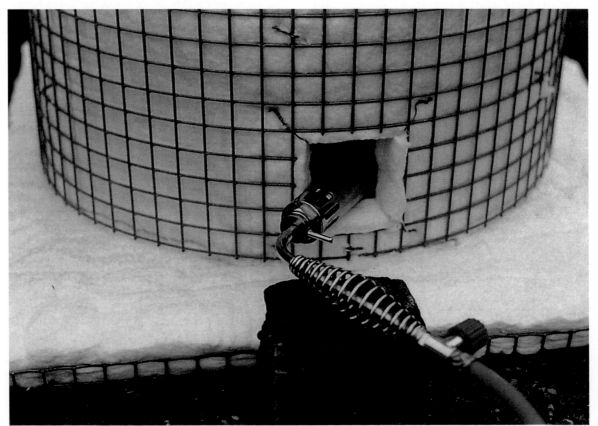

J oy Bosworth kiln: Showing the burner – a plumber's blowtorch.

the mesh and bending it over: this is the frame-work, and now it must be lined with coarse refractory ceramic fibre. Attach the fibre to the frame with ceramic buttons and nichrome wire. This kiln is fired using a plumber's blowtorch – however, as you can see, there is no flame failure device, so *extreme care* must be taken in low-lying, sheltered conditions, particularly where there are drains, when any leakage of gas could lead to an explosion. Note, too, that there is no restraint for the burner to prevent its being accidentally kicked: this might be remedied by means of a bracket on the side of the kiln – this will fix the burner in place and at the right angle for the flame. (It is always a good precaution to secure a loose burner with a heavy brick.)

Flat-Pack Kiln

Ian Gregory has devised a very simple and adaptable method of packing and firing a Raku

*I*an Gregory's flat-pack kiln (above).

*I*an Gregory's flat-pack kiln showing the bag-wall composed of an old kiln shelf.

*I an Gregory: a firing
in the flat-pack kiln
(below).*

*I an Gregory's kiln,
dry-built from 'Durox'
blocks (right).*

kiln. He has taken four sheets of weldmesh and attached fibre with buttons and nichrome wire; there is an inner face of foil (the type used behind central heating radiators). The fibre is sprayed on its hot face with rigidizer, and the soft edges butted together to create a seal. The work is built on a plinth made from firebrick. Finally it is allowed to dry out thoroughly. For the bisque firing the four sides of the kiln are erected like a box around the piece and held in place with large clips (large jump-lead clips

devices so they can fire a large work without having to move it. Inspired by a 'rotary clothes drier', their prototype works as follows: they can raise the lid and, with one of the arms, expose the red-hot work; metal sheets are then placed around the base of the work to hold back some of the heat. Next a hollow tube, an

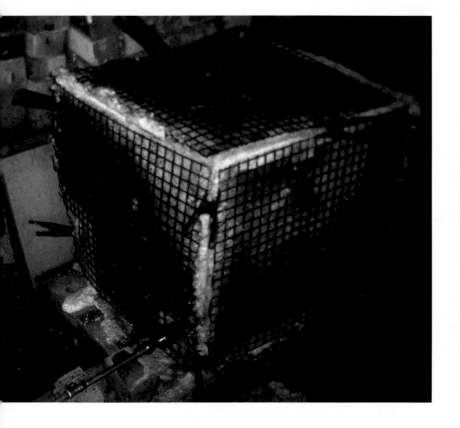

might be used). Another sheet is placed over the top as a lid; this can be moved to control the draught. The piece is fired slowly.

For Raku firing the piece is glazed and then placed on the plinth, and the kiln assembly process is repeated. Any of the panels can be removed to allow access to the ceramic.

Kiln to Fire Large Work Without Moving It

Peter Hayes and his family have designed and built a top-hat kiln with a series of lifting

open-ended oil-drum, is lowered over the piece, and a plastic bag of sawdust is clipped to another arm and swung over the still hot pot; the heat rising from the work melts the thin plastic and the sawdust falls into the tube and reduces the ceramic. The tube is raised after about ten minutes, and the copper surface of the piece is then 'painted' with a blowtorch, alternately heating it and waiting for the colours to develop, then freezing them with a spray of water (*see* pages 7, 8, 68 and 69).

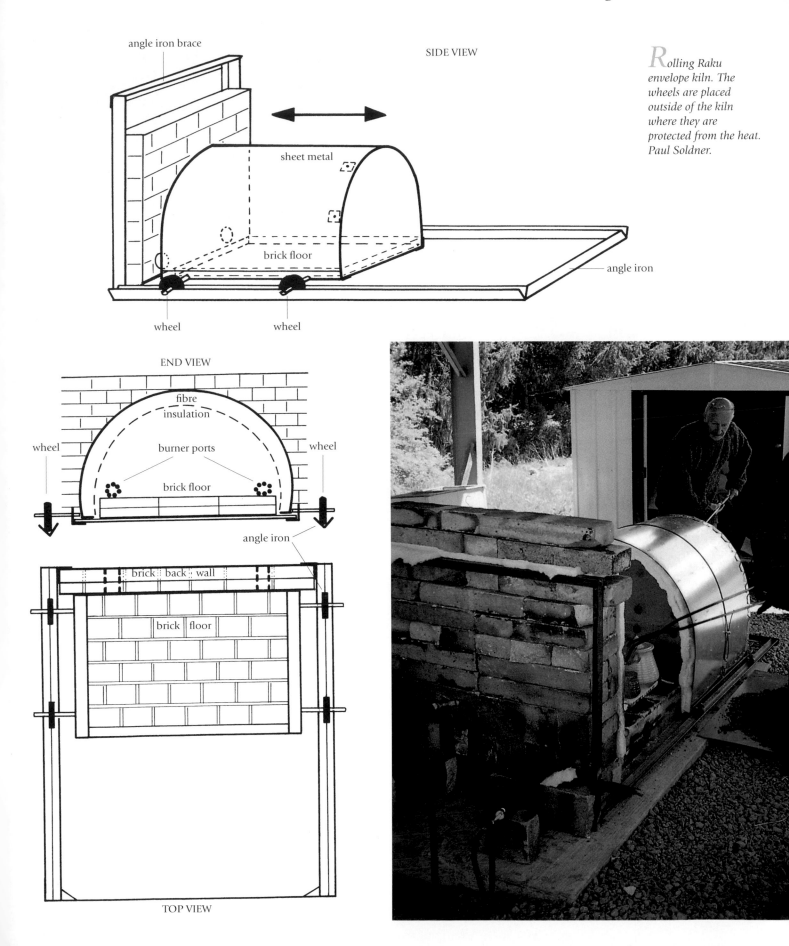

angle iron brace

SIDE VIEW

sheet metal

brick floor

angle iron

wheel   wheel

*R*olling *Raku envelope kiln. The wheels are placed outside of the kiln where they are protected from the heat. Paul Soldner.*

END VIEW

fibre insulation

wheel

burner ports

wheel

brick floor

angle iron

brick   back   wall

brick   floor

TOP VIEW

Peter Hayes kiln firing:

Top-hat kiln and counterbalances (right).

The kiln lid is lifted and removed to reveal the glowing pot (far right).

A steel drum is lowered over the pot, and sawdust is dropped from another arm (below).

The steel drum in place over the pot, and sawdust is deposited on the work (below right).

Rachel Hayes wearing a rebreathing face mask to protect her from the smoke (above left).

'Painting' with a blowtorch (don't try this at home!) (above).

Freezing copper lustre with water (left).

(All photographs by Rod Dorling.)

Developments From Post-Firing Reduction

The range of secondary reduction materials encompasses much of the vegetable kingdom: sawdust, wood shavings, straw, grain, fruit skins, specific leaves – all of these can be fresh or dried. A number of these materials have been employed actually in contact with the pot in the kiln, and the vapours held in place by a ceramic container: a saggar. The simplest saggar is a sawdust kiln.

Vessel decorated with terra sigillata and sawdust fired, Magdalene Odundo.

Sawdust Firing

Often this box is not actually fired inside the kiln itself but as a free-standing structure: a sawdust kiln. The temperatures achieved are relatively low and so it is possible to use a metal-walled vessel or a brick-built structure. The main problems that I have found are: that it is hard to ignite sawdust in the first place (solution: put in a few blocks of paraffin, or use the liquid barbecue

Packing pit firing, Ray Rogers (right).

lighting fuel); flaring, as a wind takes hold and causes the sawdust to flame – this uneven heating can cause the clay to crack. To avoid this, tighten up all those gaps in the structure which had been left to allow sufficient draught for the sawdust to be ignited. Then be patient: you must allow the kiln to cool sufficiently before removing the blackened objects. Everyone who has done a number of sawdust or Raku firings will have had experience with damp sawdust at some time or another. Instead of contour lines left as the sawdust burns down, there are swirls and halos, where the hot steam and vegetable oils and juices have penetrated the pot.

Pit Firing

Heat is retained and the flames directed by the earth walls of a trench cut through the soil. Bisque pots are placed on a bed of sawdust and inter-

spersed with woods, pine needles, salt, copper, and mineral-rich leaves such as cabbage, rhubarb or banana skins; wrapping the work with fine strands of metal such as copper wire or wire wool will give other marks. Kindling is built over the top of the pots, and the stack is ignited at the downwind end. If the timber is dry the fire will rage, but it can be 'controlled' by placing sheets of corrugated iron over the pit in order to quell the flames and control the burn until all that is left are glowing embers. After the pots are washed, one can see imprinted on the clay how and where the torrent of flame has licked over the ware: it is marked by the passage of fire. Tongues of flame are seemingly frozen into the ceramic in patterns of black and grey and pink and white. Vegetables contain quantities of the fluxing material potassium and many (colouring) trace elements such as iron, manganese and copper. The best colour development comes on white clay; on iron-bearing clays the colours are more subdued and subtler. To duplicate this artificially, or enhance it chemically, we sprinkle the soluble salts of our colouring materials around the work, or soak wood in solutions of those salts, namely iron chloride, cobalt nitrate, copper sulphate, manganese chloride, and so on. Common salt (sodium chloride) is another very useful material

which seems to help volatilize and intensify some of the colours.

Controlling the speed of the pit firing with corrugated iron sheets.

Completion of pit firing (left).

Saggar

Digging a trench in the ground and having one's own subterranean climbing kiln may be a possibility for the rural potter, but it is not so easy to persuade urban neighbours of the need to turn the environment into an impenetrable choking fog. These effects can also be achieved in a saggar in a fuel-burning kiln.

Saggar in a gas kiln vented to the outside, Rik Van de Wege.

Traditionally a saggar was a clay structure that was used to protect delicate ware from the staining effects of wood- or coal-burning kilns. Now saggars are used by craft potters to confine flame, chemicals and pot in intimate contact. A saggar can be built in a number of ways: from stacked refractory bricks; from a refractory clay, like one used for raku; and cardboard soaked in slip. (Paper clay saggars: *see* section on Sebastian Blackie, page 149.)

The pots are then surrounded by volatiles and combustibles from steel wool to photo-waste – it is obviously important that your kiln is well vented! One can experiment with firing temperatures from 1000°C to 1250+°C, the colours becoming subtler as the clay is fired harder. Smooth, burnished white clays are the best vehicles for colour development; red, coarse clays will impart a more muted quality.

Pot saggar fired in a gas kiln, Rik Van de Wege.

*P*orcelain pot fired with soluble salts in a saggar, Ardine Spitters.

*S*aggar-fired sculpture, Paul Riley (right).

'Fossil plate' casting
slip, and found sherd
saggar-fired with
combustibles, Liz Cave.

PAPER KILN

Environmentally sound, this kiln is constructed
from rolled newspapers over a willow frame-
work. It can burn very fast, so it can be useful to
have a slip 'coat' to place over the kiln to slow
the combustion.

Self-Firing Structure

Nina Hole has evolved a modular system of construction using a simple 'building block':

> The blocks are made from 'U'-shaped slabs
> about the size of a small firebrick, with one leg
> longer than the other. The blocks are then
> stacked one on top of the other, with the open
> ends alternating. The system is amazingly
> strong and can easily support a three-metre
> high structure. The actual building blocks

create an open-weave wall which allows for fast
drying and quick firing. It is a natural consequence of my life with Raku that has challenged
me to unveil this kind of sculpture. One of the
basic ideas was to involve a lot of people,
because that combination of working and
building together is a wonderful learning
process for everybody – it gives each piece a
unique spirit, drawn from each group that
works together. The process is as important as
the final product.

The technology employed in this (ad)venture is
new, and is being invented as the projects
progress. The structure is built on a firebox; it is
gas- and wood-fired. Once the firing has com-
menced and the piece has dried out, it is
wrapped in ceramic fibre to retain some of the
heat and also to direct that heat to the bottom of
the sculpture and to fire the outside walls (protective masks are worn throughout this opera-
tion of handling fibre).

Student engaged in paper kiln construction, Sebastian Blackie (far left).

Paper kiln burning.

End of paper kiln firing.

*N*ina Hole sculpture: Kiln wrapped in a fibre blanket (right).

*F*inished kiln sculpture (below). (See also page 150).

*F*iring process of stone and clay sculpture 'On Line', Michael Scheuermann (below right). (See also page 152).

They see the limitations imposed on them as creative obstacles to be overcome, and thereby to have developed their thought beyond that problem. As Nina says: 'The process does constrain our creativity and therefore provides a tremendous artistic challenge – the constraint is part of the inspiration. We have been experimenting with different fireboxes that dictate the basic structure of the type of sculpture that will be built.'

Thus the work is conceived from the bottom up, and the top down, the design of the firebox determining the structure above, which in its turn predicates a certain design for the heating chamber.

4 The Search for Ideas

Aeons ago, when hunters first paused from the chase and took time to reflect on their own existence and that of their prey, we assume that there was no distinction between hunting and art. It is suggested that the artists depicting the hunted animal on the walls of a cave using earth pigments were in fact the hunters themselves, and that there was no separation in their lives between the two activities.

However, as the division of labour within a society became increasingly role-orientated, that of the artist became more of a vocation. Potters creating vessels as receptacles for food satisfied a basic human requirement, and by the nineteenth century European hand-made pots were largely mass produced. Today, when a clay artist can make whatever he or she chooses, it is sometimes surprisingly difficult to get initial ideas, or to discover a rationale for the work.

The Research Endeavour

Why, how, and where do we find new ideas for design and artistic creation? Creative work in ceramics can start from what we may call 'process': that is, the question 'How do we do it?' can lead into the reason why we make something. Thus we can look closely at methods of manufacture, modes of firing and ways of decorating, and these will lead us to a new means of expression.

Alternatively, the stimuli for our ideas can come from deliberate research, either as a response to nature, or to 'human-made' objects in the world. These can be from the ceramic tradition, or found objects that have no obvious relationship to the history of clay. Natural objects can have a direct relationship to the outcome: for instance the relationship between the human or animal form and figurative sculpture, or a very indirect one, for instance, that between landscape and the surface of a thrown pot. Research can lead one to discover inspiration in museums. The direct observation of those artefacts through photography and sketching can enable us to 'possess' them for ourselves.

Synthesis

The 'how' of the research endeavour explores ways in which an object is made, and then applies that knowledge to one's own work. Certainly the history of ceramic is littered with examples of learning through imitation (mimesis). Some of the earliest clay pots are imitative of baskets, and some of the early Chinese wares copy bronze objects.

In our century the most prominent source has been that of Chinese and Japanese ceramic history held up as an example of excellence by Bernard Leach. The Chinese pot became an icon almost slavishly copied by his followers. And yet what is clear from Leach's own output is that he combined the Oriental ideal with the medieval English slipware tradition to fashion a new vocabulary. This practice of 'synthesis', of combining and modifying one or more traditions, is central to my exposition in this chapter.

Raku-fired pot based on a Chinese ginger jar, Mel Brown.

A CONTINUOUS LEARNING CURVE

Ceramics is dominated by a mystique of technique and materials. Part of the reason is that many pottery methodologies are apparently simple, and yet they are infuriatingly difficult to get right, needing time and practice; nonetheless, there is a feeling that all that is required is a magic bullet. At pottery demonstrations there is always a plethora of questions – What temperature? What is the glaze recipe that you are using? – and they are often based on the assumption that there are secrets that the cognoscenti are keeping from the rest of us. It also seems to be assumed that if these secrets can be winkled out, then it will be possible to produce work such as the demonstrator produces. Of course, the truth is that we can't; but we can certainly learn from public presentations of skill, finesse and the application of ideas. I would like to suggest that nowadays what we learn is not so much how to make a particular pot or figure, but rather how we can approach a problem and realize a solution. This is as near as most of us get to continuous apprenticeship; the solutions posed are not the way to make a teapot or a sculpture in the style of so and so, but rather a way of tackling a particular problem that can be adopted and used in our own work. Thus the way that a spout is attached to a body may also be an insight into how one attaches the foot of a figure to its leg.

ASSIMILATING A METHODOLOGY

Watching an expert in his or her field can be a very passive exercise; in fact what is necessary is not just observation but rather assimilation through borrowing/acquiring/stealing/owning/processing and practice. This can be an unconscious activity: in a fairly unreflective way we home in on a process or a methodology and start working in that genre, perhaps as a result of the pressure that our teachers put us under, perhaps because of other external necessities. However, at some point in our development we need to stop and to reassess, and then one can actively identify a skill or a process that is needed, and unashamedly steal it and make it one's own. But after a while our personality will shine through, as the process or technique is taken into our own repertoire; there is no fixed 'right' way to do anything, what we are looking for is a way that suits us the best. When watching a demonstration one is aiming at a distillation of experience: the first temptation may be to brazenly imitate, but what should be held uppermost in the mind is that any learning is for the future when a new interpretation will be given to the methodology.

This emphasis on 'how?', on skill, seems at variance with some contemporary fine art practice, in which the focus on *concept* seems to be growing; consequently the number of practitioners who do not *make* is also on the increase. Sometimes this is akin to the kind of delegation that occurred in former times, wherein Giotto or Henry Moore would develop an idea and other artisans/artists would execute it. Then there is art by assemblage, for instance in the work of Kurt Schwitters, which is a different type of alchemy to the transformation of raw material and the fashioning of form. Artists take and juxtapose objects, and suggest through the specific linking that they have established a new way of seeing and a new way of looking at an idea. One of the main ways that one can identify this difference is in the titling of artefacts.

Often in ceramics one feels that a title for a work is superfluous, because its meaning is intuited from sharing its presence, rather than being conceptually given and acquired. Often when a clay artist gives a piece of work a title it is merely descriptive – for example 'Jug'. It can of course be a helpful indication as to what inspired the potter – say, Stone Age weapons; and it can be a glance offered inside the mask of ideas behind which other potters may wish to hide.

Resources: Where to Research

The *where* of the research endeavour involves the storehouses of human knowledge. In most cities there are collections of pottery, sculpture or painting, good repositories of information, in the great museums, and for those of us who do not have access to art galleries then obviously books can play a similar role. The other major source of images and information is the world-wide web, and more and more of the museums are putting their collections 'on line'. Most teachers, however, advocate that objects of interest should be directly observed; and artefacts that might be used for artistic stimulation can be collected at home – for instance, the sea-shells and weathered wood of our holiday travels.

Critical Philosophy: The Artist's Motivation

The *why* of a search for new ideas is an issue of much more recent provenance (as it is in the disciplines of Fine Art as well as in the crafts). In the past a potter would be indentured as an apprentice or would follow in a parent's footsteps and make the time-honoured forms with an established mode of decoration and firing that suited the function of their work and also its market: one has a notion of generations of unknown craftsmen producing a great deal of work, often

*P*rimal bowl with weapon artefact, Raku-fired, Rick Hirsch.

of great sensitivity, but behaving almost unreflectingly in their observance of the best and most ergonomic way to achieve their ends. Now, however, mechanization and industrialization have liberated the craftsman from the dull routine of churning out objects as fast as possible, and he or she now has time to dwell on outcomes. Once it is recognized that there is a freedom in terms of product, then there is also time to contemplate aesthetic questions such as the artist's motivation, and why the piece produced might be considered to be a 'good' object even if it doesn't appear to function very well.

THE LEGACY OF HISTORY

The way that something is made or fired does not make us think just of the pot in front of us, but also all of the pots that have been finished in that way in the past. Furthermore they are not merely called to mind, they are also available to be commented upon by a contemporary potter. In the eye of the public, a hand-made pot is generally identified by the traces left by the potter's wheel and the more sensuous marks left by his fingers and hands; an additional repertory is provided by mark-making tools, which can complement those left by the fingers or actually stand in for them. These are traces that, after firing, remain like a fossil – atavistic marks from the past – for eternity. I am sure that many potters have dug through the remains of an old kiln site and when picking up some ancient vessel have been aware that they are perhaps only the second person to put their hands in the grooves where, a thousand years ago, the original artisan left his mark. The maker is long ago forgotten, but for the handprints. The marks are spirals, emanating from the base of a pot and ending at the rim: they speak of skill, speed and spontaneity – not big, loud gestures, but intimate movements, trapped forever.

It is the Japanese clay tradition that has elevated these accidental marks into a fluent language of manipulation. The slow wheel and soft clay captures every nuance of the process, from wiping with a sponge to trimming with a bamboo tool; from different ways of removing surplus clay to a whole variety of textures that are left after pulling up the clay, including of course the marks left as it is removed from the wheel-head. In our century these are qualities and expressionistic devices that have been exploited by Peter Voulkos. He stacked wet and leather-hard forms that he had taken from the wheel to create hubristic expressions of his energy – in direct opposition to the concepts underpinning the tea ceremony wares that encouraged a restrained and quiet mode of expression. However, there was actually nothing self-effacing about the sensibilities of the original tea masters and their patrons: they just shouted very quietly and everyone had to strain forward to listen.

LEARNING FROM OUR PREDECESSORS: REFERENCING IDEAS

I have a very strong sense in my own work of referencing traditions, by far the most important and significant being that of the tea-ceremony vessels. Incidentally I have found that this is not the case with many Raku potters, a fact which originally quite surprised me. Coming to ceramics in a roundabout route has made me very keen to investigate the ceramic tradition in England, particularly as I have always believed very strongly in the necessity to be aware of the work of my predecessors, not just so that I can learn from them and avoid some of the easy mistakes that can be made, but also so that I can hold their achievements in my mind's eye and effect a commentary on their history. I find it very useful to have an understanding of the Raku tradition, which itself is not just a range of pots but also a philosophical response to clay. This is captured in the range of actions that are predicated by those vessels, both in their manufacture and use. Most Raku potters that I have talked with do not actually consider the tea-ceremony philosophy of *wabi* and *sabi* to have a significance for them, and pay scant regard to it in their statements. However, I shall endeavour to indicate in the following chapters how this sensibility is very important as an unconscious constituent of their work.

REFERENCING PROCESS

The sense of referencing referred to above is not merely to do with the ideas behind the work, but can also be concerned with process, for instance *fire* as in the work of Stephen Charnock.

The immediate and very obvious physical stuff of manufacture – clay – can also be seen as significant because it echoes that early coarse fabric utilized by Japanese masters. My clay is

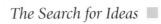

Found and photographed charred wood, Stephen Charnock.

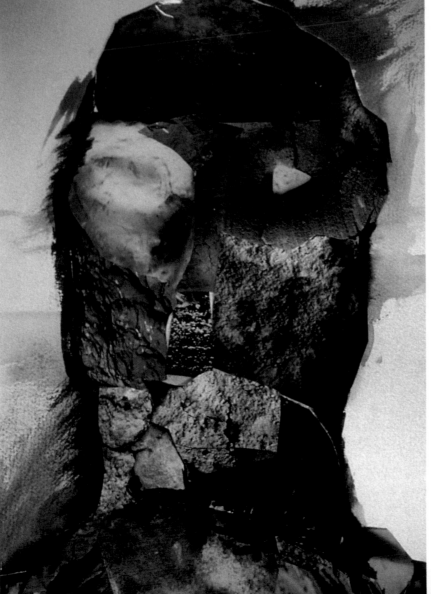

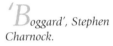
'Boggard', Stephen Charnock.

apparently gritty and rough, even though it is a sophisticated version of their body; however, it performs the same function for me in that it has very low thermal expansion. It can certainly look like one of these clays, as it has a very high proportion of ground, calcined (pre-fired) clay in its make-up. It is, though, very smooth for throwing and has remarkable properties of tensile strength, making it a perfect clay for throwing thin or thick, and for removing red hot from the kiln. Thus the notion of referencing is largely an attitude of mind, as most Raku potters are trying to achieve a similar goal, namely of work

measured by perfection and symmetry, but by its organic and naturally evolved sensibility: you could go so far as to say that it celebrates the idea of the world as incomplete and imperfect. The rim undulates, and is quite distinct from the exact edge of a china cup; it is a series of falls and rises that guides the mouth to the best of all depressions on the rim from which to drink. This is a motif that I have investigated at length: it is a device that leads the eye around the pot, quite unlike the straight, flat track of the commercial cup which does not allow for this guidance – we rely on a succession of images on the

*C*rushed *tin can. (Photograph by David Jones.)*

without cracks. It is an attitude of mind that can also inform the choice of objects to be made.

Tea-ceremony ware has developed a rarified aesthetic over its four centuries of manufacture, and a number of its facets are significant in my own output: for instance, acute attention is paid to the rim of a vessel. The original reference is to objects that the artist has experienced – perhaps the outline of a high mountain range or a rock pool – so the success of, say, a tea bowl is not

surface to do this for us. It is also a journey that is effected by the hands, in that the fingers turn a good tea bowl, the hands informing the eye of the right way to hold it.

My own pots reference the throwing process very precisely. It is a technique that primarily interests me because it is a spontaneous way of creating, though it has additional significance in that it is associated in the public mind as the defining pottery-making technique – the result

of centuries of domestic pottery production and the 'brown mug revolution' of the 1970s. So the thrown vessel is like a comment on current and historical pottery practice. What is it precisely that I want to say? To begin with we might consider the dominion of the symmetrical and circular: in the popular mind pots have always been, or aspired to be, round. However, it is the legacy of the expressionist clay deformers in California (Voulkos, Reitz, *et al.*) and the reformers of post-Bauhaus Europe (Rie and Coper) that pottery has moved away from this, and throwing has been liberated as a very creative discipline.

There are other (hand-building) techniques which can also adopt signature quality, because they remind us of process. Much hand assembly of clay involves the utilization of modular elements, and these combine to form

a rhythm that can instantly identify a particular artist's work.

REFERENCING FORM AND PATTERN

As well as method, the past possesses a wealth of form and pattern that we can plunder, and the cliche 'it's all been done before' only serves to remind us that it is going to be a rich vein. It is also one which contains a warning about stealing bravely, but disguising the theft! (Unless it involves a sense of post-modern referencing.) So how do we set about this task? At our disposal are two major sources of imagery. The so-called 'primary' source objects are found in personally owned collections, or socially owned museums – thus even if we are not sufficiently fortunate to have a Ming vase in our inheritance to study,

'Alice's cup and saucer', deconstructed spoon, David Jones. (Photograph by Rod Dorling.)

Drawing of a monkey, Emma Rodgers.

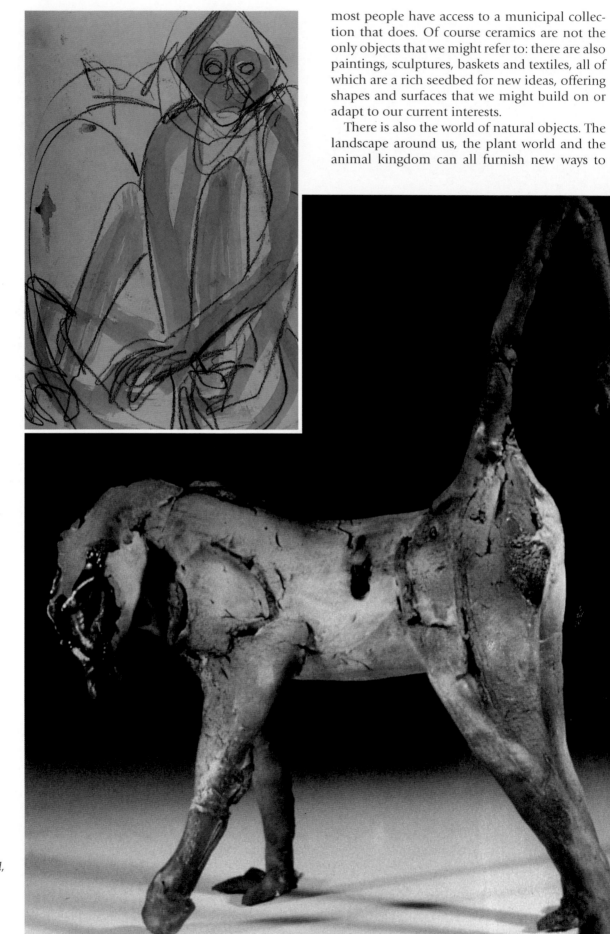

most people have access to a municipal collection that does. Of course ceramics are not the only objects that we might refer to: there are also paintings, sculptures, baskets and textiles, all of which are a rich seedbed for new ideas, offering shapes and surfaces that we might build on or adapt to our current interests.

There is also the world of natural objects. The landscape around us, the plant world and the animal kingdom can all furnish new ways to

Baboon, Raku-fired, Emma Rodgers.

handle, impress, paint and fashion clay. Then there are all the other objects to be discovered in the man-made environment, both in the town and in the country.

Carrying a camera in order to photograph things of interest can provide both a general documentation and an analytic understanding of an object. Sketching gives a greater familiarity and is an even better way to generate new ideas as it involves a longer time and more persistent hard looking. Alternatively there are books: many are now lavishly illustrated and full of pictures of objects that one might like to make.

So, what does one do to avoid making objects identical to those illustrated? This in itself is a fairly new question, firstly because the history of clay has always been one of tradition – pots being made in the image of the father's or mother's pots. As a craftsman one was *meant* to make ceramic objects like the exemplars of a previous generation: originality was not revered as a quality of pottery. Secondly, clay has always been used as a mimetic material – that is, one employed to imitate other substances. The history of ceramics is full of examples of pots being created like squashes, or bamboo or cauliflowers; and early Chinese boxes were often made in imitation of bronze ones.

'Visual Thinking'

Investigating the Means of Manufacture

A number of tricks can be used to encourage the modern artist to look closely at objects from the historical tradition and then to modify the researches. One of my favourite projects I call 'In the style of …': this involves identifying any object from ceramic history and then making it as accurately as possible. The kind of tasks you could attempt might be to research in depth the glazing techniques required to make a Tang horse or a Kenzan bowl, and to look at the concomitant making techniques. There again a Hans Coper vessel or a Ron Nagle cup might be the focus.

This is analogous to sketching and copying paintings by the Old Masters in art galleries: by investigating the means of manufacture a deeper understanding is reached, one which is infinitely more profound than just reading about

how to do something – it is a form of learning through doing. This is the old mechanism of handing down knowledge in the crafts – it is like the master demonstrating and the apprentice copying. Our agenda, though, is not to get an exact copy, but to take this learning and to

'*M*argerita', *Raku-fired ceramic, Michael Flynn.*

personalize it; it is important that the student brings something of himself to the activity. (This is the sea-change that has occurred in the Crafts, where in previous generations individuality and idiosyncrasy were not encouraged, and were perhaps even frowned upon.)

'Joan of Arc', Sue Halls.

Analysis and Representation

The next stage is one of analysis, whereby the piece is broken down via a series of sketches and doodles; or it may be reinterpreted in another material such as cardboard, or in a collage with fabric, or an assemblage with found materials, and so on and so forth. This is a process of

abstraction. The earliest examples of this mode of interpreting the world are the cave drawings found at prehistoric sites (these drawings, incidentally, are made with coloured clays on the cave wall); it is an art of representation and not of an exact attempt at cloning. We live in a postmodern world of comment and irony, but it seems we can identify the beginnings of today's distancing process taking place in the past as the nomadic hunters retreated deep into caves in a French mountain and drew their prey animals. We assume that this had a magical intention, namely to capture the spirit of the beast – in art form it allowed itself to be caught by the pursuer; and this is much as the modern artist looks to capture the essence of a creature, perhaps to comment on our own animal ancestry. Yet such painting also functions for us as a commentating device on the environment of those artists.

Collage

Collage is a very useful technique to get the mind working in an allusive way. All the time we are looking for new ways of saying things, but perhaps we try too hard. At the present time one could say that there is an over-emphasis on the conscious as the way ideas come about, and collage can, to an extent, circumvent this and facilitate a more unconscious way of thinking. Collage was used early this century by the artist Kurt Schwitters to make objects for exhibition. Nowadays it is one of the standard tools used by artists to access new ways of seeing, and new ways of examining unconscious attitudes to visual constructs and concepts. Schwitters assembled bits of his personal world and fashioned them into artefacts that had qualities of proportion and scale and yet told of his own unique experiences. One can use this methodology in a similar way: by using personal materials one can examine a form and create a new view of an icon.

Collage can also be utilized to progress from the two-dimensional nature of a drawing or photograph, via the intermediate mode of low-relief collage, to a three-dimensional piece. Thus a familiar form is analysed and manipulated using junk and any of the materials familiar from children's TV art programmes – cardboard tubes, corrugated paper, torn card, coloured magazine pictures, metal stampings, and so on. This is a 'freeing-up' technique, in which assumptions about the nature and structure of, say, a baboon, a teacup or the human figure are not merely set aside but are also subverted, as the new materials are employed not merely to look again at the structure of the object, but to get closer to its essential nature. Ideally one can then perceive these qualities in a new way for oneself. It is possible to set up this exercise to

create a range of objects that are quite different to the starting point: thus a rock formation can become a tall pot, a plate, a wall structure or a six-foot-high teapot.

An *openness of mind*, admitting of a multiplicity of solutions, is the best attitude from which to start. This state is analagous to the desired end of Zen meditation – a state underlying the practice of 'tea ceremony'.

'Scream', Raku-fired with colloidal slip, Sue Halls.

Joy Bosworth collage.

'High-rise teapot', Raku-fired, Dennis Farrell (far right). (Compare page 95.)

The Relevance of Raku Philosophy

It certainly is the case that ordinary clay utensils have other functions beyond their use, and it is in this area that Raku and tea-ceremony philosophy become so relevant. These pots were apparently created just to hold food, flowers and drink, but there is much evidence from contemporary anthropology that pots do have a *significance* in their usage. Pots communicate coded messages: it may be the overt expression of wealth or social status – an ornate footring is a sure sign of affluence; or it may be the intimate relationship between a husband and wife, indicating desire and availability for intercourse – the inversion of a bedside pot (cited by Nigel Barley in 'Smashing Pots'). By and large a lot of the subtlety of this coding has been lost in the West, and we are left solely with economic determinants; however, this shouldn't prevent us from gazing further into the aesthetic transactions that take place when viewing ceramic and evolving a decoding system (*see also Ceramics* by Philip Rawson).

*D*rawing of fruit, Mari Oda (right).

*P*hotograph of folded body, Mari Oda.

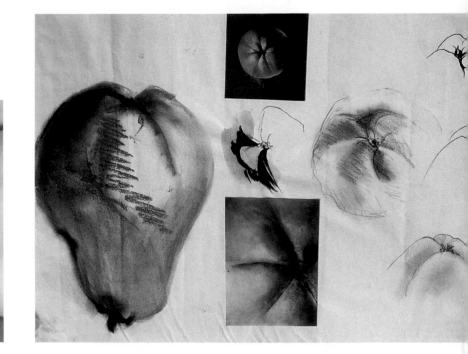

'*B*arefoot walk', Mari
Oda. (See also *page 115*.)

*D*rawing based on a found tray, Joy Bosworth.

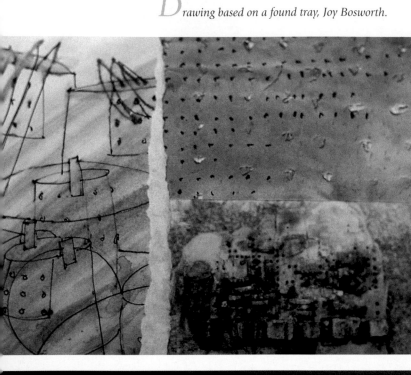

*F*ound perforated tray, Joy Bosworth (above).

*R*aku-fired tray with gold leaf decoration, Joy Bosworth.

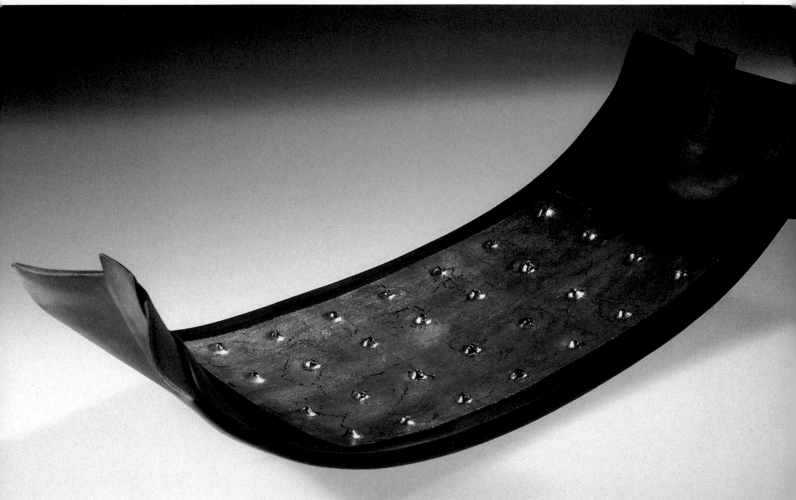

Pattern and Embellishment

One of the features of human artefacts is pattern and embellishment – indeed we particularly notice objects that do not carry these qualities because we isolate them and call them 'minimalist (*see* page 126)'. At some levels it is surprising to see just *how* much time is obviously invested in objects made by people leading a subsistence way of life in order to decorate them. This pattern-making can develop from an interest in, and observation of, the natural world around the potters.

Thus drawing and redrawing a tracery of ivy around a pot can lead to a geometric pattern, and it is possible to interpret this not just as a drawn line on a hard surface, but also as, say, an

*S*ketch of wash-hand basin, Ros Ingram.

*R*aku-fired fountain, Ros Ingram.

Large Raku-fired jar, Lidia Zavadsky.

incised line in soft clay. Furthermore, we can extend and re-invent our definition of tools; in this way what we consider to be the detritus of our twentieth-century urban society – cogs and car mats, rusted metal and disused clothing – can all become means of achieving texture.

These marks can be reinterpreted again using home-made equipment – for instance metal combs and forks employed to gouge lines, car mats turned into plaster moulds in order to create complexity of surface. There are many other different ways in which line can be applied in clay: it can be painted in glaze or slip, it can be incised and stamped, or built up with coils of soft clay or torn fragments; all of these give different qualities of surface. One should develop a repertoire of marks in clay and also a reinterpretation of these in a sketchbook; this latter is an essential place for collecting and processing information. Photographic images can be incorporated into the sketchbook via a photocopier, stuck down and reinterpreted either in pencil sketches or in collage. Thus a filtered version of general experience can become the foundation for a personal truth.

Narrative and Personal Style

Ideas, narratives and ways of working combine together to form the basis of personal style. Narrative used as the basis of a body of work can be simply illustrative or more complexly allusive: that is, one can remake an ancient myth; or one might wish to bring it up to date – as in the iconography of Michael Flynn (*see* pages 85, 131–2) who weaves a ceramic web around stories, myths and legends. One can also see in the work of Lydia Zavadsky the referencing of the archaic pots dug up in Israel.

Installation is beginning to attract many clay artists as a means of expression, and can be stimulated by ideas based on concepts of minimalism, architectural theory and numerology. These are ideas that are bleeding across into the domain of ceramic, and specifically in our case Raku, from sculpture and other Fine Art concerns.

So what are the determinants of style? It is an interesting question to ask – we could almost look at it as a notion of how we develop a personal handwriting. At the very least we know that with the demise of the guild system, an artisan's work is no longer made (God-like) in the image of the master's.

5 Raku and Low Fire Today

During the last three decades, Raku and other low-temperature firing techniques have progressed from being merely interesting sideline (and side-show) activities to being mainstream technologies for the making of ceramic. As a process Raku is fascinating for demonstrating how a glaze sinters, melts and runs; and sawdust-firing raw clay can demonstrate in a very simple way how clay can be converted to ceramic. But the question is: how can this knowledge be harnessed for the creation of contemporary work, and why have Raku and low-firing techniques been selected as such popular ways of firing?

During the past thirty years a variety of authors have tried to illustrate how potters respond to clay and low temperature firing. Some of the potters featured in these books are familiar as practitioners who have been actively engaged with Raku since those early readings of *A Potter's Book*. I have included new work by some of these artists, and featured other practitioners who are newcomers, and some who are students (from the Ceramics Department at the University of Wolverhampton); all of them have chosen Raku or related techniques in their search for a personal language with which to express their ideas, finding in it a quality that 'feels right' or in some way answers the questions that they see posed in their work. There are also those artists who have tried Raku and then moved to quite other modes of expression, taking with them traces of what they learnt in Raku.

I would like to discuss the work of the artists participating in this book in the context of Raku and low fire, not simply as a way of finishing a piece, but essentially as a way of thinking and also as an inspiration for form. In addition, Raku seems to be an ideal way of considering issues of metaphor and of examining process in

clay, and thereby leading back to an investigation of fire itself.

I have categorized the work in four sections, which illustrate the most significant themes in Raku and low fire today. They are as follows:

1: The Allusive

In Raku one can perceive two broad strands of allusion, or reference: there is the reference to other cultural traditions and their artefacts, and there is also the mythopoeic use of the ritual of fire. Ceramic is the material on which our first writings are recorded; it is also an ancient building material, and it has long been associated with food and cooking. It is also a favourite material for containing our remains after our death. The process of firing and secondary reduction seems to refer indirectly to archaeology, rebirth and initiation: the work enters the kiln pristine, although untested in a sacramental sense; it is then dug out of ash, sawdust and carbon, like an ancient artefact; and it must be cleansed and washed before the artist allows the piece to go out into the world. These echoes of the archaic and of ritual are emphasized in work that deals directly with the objects of the Raku tradition, as well as work that evokes the past.

Potters also allude to other cultural traditions pertaining to vessels, art or tools. For many of today's potters this is a post-modern sifting activity, born of conscious choice – it is not just the blind following of a tradition. For instance, one way of developing ideas for Raku might be in extending an acknowledged body of work, such as the tea ceremony; other ways involve the splicing and juxtaposing of influences from disparate sources: this polyglot sampling is seen clearly in Rick Hirsch's vessels.

This allusion to other cultures is a process that leads towards the objects that have no obvious referent. These I chose to classify as the 'Metaphoric'.

2: The Metaphoric

This is a category where the object stands for a feeling or form beyond the one that we immediately see before us. In some sense almost all contemporary, non-functional ceramics will fall into this category, seeming to stand outside any tradition and to be emancipated from anything that has gone before – though it may well be possible for viewers to discern the roots of these pieces, which may express great formal complexity, or embody minimalist modernist concerns.

3: The Representational

Recently there has been a resurgence of interest in *the figure*, both human and animal, as a form for artistic interpretation; this mirrors a similar shift in contemporary painting and sculpture away from the abstract. I would suggest that one of the reasons for the choice of Raku or sawdust as firing processes for figurative work is a combination of the practical with the mystic. By leaving the clay surface marked only by smoke and fire one feels closer to the essence of the subject, or more literally the body; there are no clothes of glaze to hide behind, only the bare, vulnerable clay skin. But on the other hand, the use of Raku glaze and the dynamic nature of the firing can imply the energy and vigour of life.

4: The Processial

This is work that references the way that the object has come into being as its own major theme. So there is work that references the wet clay stage, decoration and particularly fire.

Contemporary Responses: The Allusive

Dennis Farrell

Dennis Farrell's work deals with 'the passage of time and change, its influence on buildings, landscape and the human environment'. It acts as a mediator between past and present: 'The process of archaeology and its concern with time as layers which contain evidence of the past has greatly influenced the way in which I express my ideas. Architectural fragments, marks on the landscape, the layers and patterns of wallpaper revealed in the demolition of old houses have become source material for ceramic objects with a timeless feel.'

Farrell's work relates to the frequently perceived disjunction between the grand, cultural statement and the individual, personal experience, and responds to it by using familiar, domestic pottery forms to express a feeling for the landscape and history. In his words: 'The teapot is a vessel of our culture and represents comfort, refreshment and hospitality. I have used it to parody the environments in which it is used, particularly the imposing industrial architecture of Lancashire and Yorkshire. The teapot and architecture are synthesized to create stacked multi-storey forms with many layered surfaces collected from this time-worn past.'

The main historical influence on the work is the pottery of the sixteenth- and seventeenth-century Japanese artists, many of whom were making work for the tea ceremony; these include 'Oribe with its striking combination of quiet glazed and freely patterned areas, and the painterly style of the eighteenth-century potter Ogata Kenzan.' The work is thrown and altered; it is decorated using slips and underglaze colours, and the pots are bisqued and fired using either Raku or related saggar techniques. In Raku 'the areas that received the glaze preserve the layered surface treatments, whilst the crackle effect tempers the intensity of the coloured stains. By contrast the smoked areas mute the effect of the slip and underglaze to varying degrees.' In packing the saggar kiln, the post-firing reduction material – sawdust – is placed in a saggar with the pots and small packages of salt. Too heavy a reduction is avoided by protecting the clay with sand, aluminium foil or clay pads applied to the surface. Both the saggar and Raku kilns are fired to approximately 1000°C.

'*S*tacking cups', saggar-fired teapot, Dennis Farrell. (See also *page 88.*)

Peter Hayes

Peter Hayes and his family perform a 'Medicine Show' version of Raku: they seem to have imbibed an American Wild West notion of Raku, combining a flamboyance in the firing with cool precision in the final object. They push the frontiers of the discipline. This is true 'experimentation' and *controlled* danger, though underneath lies an aesthetic impelled by a feeling of restraint, resulting in a minimalist, organic sculpture which evokes the standing stones of an unknown primitive world with an unknowable religion. Peter Hayes' ceramic sensibility combines elements of Western Raku with African bush-firing. He lived for some years in Lesotho where he observed the local potters bonfire-firing their ware; and in his first exhibition back in England he showed pots reduced in dung!

Standing stones with a gold circle, Raku-fired, Peter Hayes.

Totem retrieved from the River Avon showing the growth of copper salts (right).

*W*ater sculpture in a
Japanese garden,
Marlborough.

The clay he uses is a smooth stoneware; it has very poor thermal shock resistance. The work is constructed from textured slabs: these slabs are stretched by throwing them onto a board, where they pick up more clay and powder which have been sprinkled on the wood – this is repeated until the slabs have the quality of old skin. They are then fired either as thick slabs, or in sections, to be assembled later into totems. The work is bound in wire (to hold it together) and then fired, brutally.

After firing, the pieces are sprayed with water to encourage cracking. Whereas most contemporary Raku artists try to minimize any cracking, the Hayes technique has precisely the contrary intention: this is Raku as a celebration of cracks, as opposed to crackle! Whereas early Japanese Raku bowls were mended, preserved and enhanced by a river of gold holding the broken sections together, Peter Hayes wants many sections of broken clay: these will be stuck back together to create the tessellated effect of a broken windscreen or ice forming on a winter lake. An epoxy-resin with powder paint additions is used for gluing and demarcating the cracks, and joining the broken elements – it is a very crude form of mending that is refined later by sanding. These pieces range in size from small table-top sculpture to some that are 2–3m (6–10ft) high: these tall pieces are stuck together with larger areas of resin. Current investigations are being conducted into combining molten glass into the work at this stage.

The pieces are made in hollow sections and assembled over a steel armature embedded in concrete; they are then filled with polyurethane foam under pressure. The clay is composed of very fine particles, and so can be easily ground and eroded by disc sanders and polishers. The entire surface is brought back to the quality of smooth stone, with a red craze pattern within, where the resin holds the small sections together. The object is smeared with a paste of copper and wallpaper adhesive, and plunged into the river by the back door. Over time the soluble copper salts migrate through the still-porous clay.

After a month or two the work is pulled from the waters, each on its own string, like amphorae from a deep-sea wreck. River slime and copper salts have grown on the piece; it is dried and repolished. This process mirrors both Japanese and American Raku practice: it is dramatic, and yet it produces objects of restraint. Post-firing reduction and water-quenching both feature as processes that donate a valuable quality to the work. There seems to be an inclusiveness and all-encompassing awareness of history that pushes the work forward into new expression.

Rick Hirsch

Rick Hirsch is another artist whose abilities have dug deep into the practice of Raku; he is also the author of the book *Raku*, published in 1975. Archaeology is central to an understanding of his work, and he also exhibits a considerable knowledge when it comes to discussing Japanese tea-ceremony ware: unlike the majority of potters, he maintains an active interest in this antecedent to contemporary Raku, acknowledging its importance in feeding his work. Yet he denies the absolute seduction of his chosen form of expression: post-firing reduction Raku. As he says:

> Everything is subservient to the finished product, and the most important thing is what the work looks like. The pots are conceived as Raku pots, and the only way to get that particular

'Primal bowl with bone artefact', low-fired glazes, sandblasted, Rick Hirsch.

*P*edestal bowl with
weapon artefact',
low-fired glazes,
lacquer, Rick Hirsch.

image is the use of this process … they are about
fire – unfired they are like incomplete sentences.

Looking at his work, that sense of painting with
flame becomes palpable (*see* above and pages 41,
79 and 98). He uses combinations of very thin
layers of *terra sigillata* and reactive washes of soluble copper products; they are fired, fumed and
refired until the object is judged 'right'.

The flowing lines and musical exploration
embodied in jazz are cited as the most important inspirational force:

I have a theme, and then I let it happen … Raku
captivates me. The performance of this improvi-
sational drama is activated by devising a series of
confrontations that culminates in challenging
dialogue. The choreography in this cliff-hanger
is mainly between the artist's expertise and
nature's forces, between predictability and
chance. The variables are extensive, which makes
individual firings distinctive. Thus each piece
seizes and reflects that specific period of action.

His study of archaeology and his collection of
archaic vessels are echoed in his tripod forms.
These are mimetic structures that follow not
only the form or function of a more expensive
item, but also embody its spirit. In this case it is

not just that clay is used to copy Chinese bronze
tripods, but he is also endeavouring to evoke the
mystery of presence found in the past, to conjure
it up by his firing. A dialogue is established
between the essential and the contingent: there
is a sense of the here and now, and some half-
lost past – the firing is not a gratuitous embellishment, but an essential part of the nature of
his work: 'I do not make a separation between
Raku and the content of my work. The fire
imprints achieved through the post-firing are
required pieces of information, vitally con-
tributing to the whole idea.' But in the ultimate
post-modern move he has recently taken the
pieces that were influenced by the Chinese
bronzes right back to their roots, by actually
casting them in bronze and bringing that
process of thinking full circle.

He has also created a new body of work that
deals with tools, though these have been
imbued with a sense of ritual that is different
from the tea-ceremony artefacts. There is an evocation of sacrifice and killing that accompanies
the work, based on jade hand-axes and roughly
executed knives that split the soft clay altars on
which they are presented. There are references in
Hirsch's work to the modernist sculptors,
Noguchi and Brancusi, who were concerned
with stacking forms and worked surfaces. Hirsch

Deconstructed teapot and jug, Raku-fired lustres, David Jones (below). (Photograph by Rod Dorling.)

'Scylla and Charybdis', Raku-fired lustres, David Jones. (Photograph by Rod Dorling.)

is likewise involved with a refining of surface – sometimes it is highlighted in its entirety, at other times it is just a small fraction. By immersing himself in the mentality of a tea aficionado Rick Hirsch seems to have established a very twentieth-century Raku practice that combines the modern with the ancient.

David Jones

For me, the tea bowl is the ultimate container; it was celebrated naked of embellishment by the tea masters and made the focus of ritual. *Cha-no-yu* is not the only ritual: there is also the taking of afternoon tea, an event with a formality that has been lost in the West, where it has degenerated into the pleasant but casual, shared afternoon 'cuppa'. This is a fairly unreflective activity of drinking, albeit an essential part of Western culture with its own associated tradition of forms. I have chosen to reinterpret not merely Japanese tea-bowls (in the widest sense) but also the icons of our own 'tea ceremony', a process first of 'deconstruction', then reconstruction. It was originally stimulated by the discovery of a tin can squashed by a car in Greece which suggested a flat, planar view of an object and led to my current reinterpretation of our tea vessels (*see* page 82). It is informed by recent developments in philosophical and architectural theory, as shown particularly in the work of Derrida and Frank Gehry.

I manipulate icons such as the teapot and the cup and saucer to investigate the nature of hold-

ing and containment. The work is thrown on the potter's wheel because that activity brings with it a quintessential pottery skill that is popularly associated with the medium. I use the marks of process left by throwing and turning the soft clay, before cutting the hard pot, to indicate some of the history of the work's inception. Like the geological record in the earth, there are suggestions of its beginnings in soft, malleable wetness, and the stages leading to its conclusion can be traced in sharp, hard broken lines.

In its decoration the work references the abrupt colour changes seen in the markings of tropical fish, whilst grids and lines echo the tim-

bers of Tudor buildings and the Shoji screens of Japanese houses. Curvilinear lines describe the contours of the ploughed countryside – running parallel, or concentric and related, these lines can also be found in Japanese gardens composed of raked stones. The Zen garden brings nature into the domestic setting of home or temple, just as contemporary pottery brings earth/clay into the home as an object of contemplation.

The quality of the fired surface depends on multiple overlays of glaze. After bisque firing I apply a graphic pattern composed of tapes and latex resists. The work is sprayed with glaze, and

'Alice's tea bowl', Raku-fired lustres, David Jones. (Photograph by Rod Dorling.)

Raku-fired vessel, Elizabeth Raeburn.

some of the resist is removed; it is then sprayed again with a different glaze. After each successive layer of glaze is applied, further layers of resist are removed until some areas of the pot have up to five oversprays of very thin glaze. The glazes contain precious metals – silver, gold and copper. I give a heavy post-firing reduction to the work by always using fresh sawdust; this results in iridescence and reads against various bare surfaces of clay: grey to black, to shiny sigillata black, to resist-slip crackle, and copper matt for a rust red.

Elizabeth Raeburn

Elizabeth Raeburn is a vessel maker whose work alludes to the modern movement; it often features a prominent, incorporate base, frequently a pedestal in the form of a high foot, dramatically setting off the bowl that it supports. This is reminiscent of the pottery of Hans Coper, in whose work there is dynamic play between forms, in the way they are inter-related and juxtaposed. This represents a complex of allusions: firstly to sculpture, which has traditionally always been supported on a separate plinth; and it reminds the viewer of the high-footed stem cups of the Ming dynasty – though Raeburn's work differs profoundly from these in that the emphasis is on the 'otherness' of the foot and the distancing effect it gives from the surface that the piece stands on.

Elizabeth's work has recently taken a new, yet parallel direction. In 1995 she won a competition to design and make a mural for a hospital in Somerset, England, and in its construction one can see that her well-honed skill in making, assembling and Raku-firing slabs of clay (for that is how she makes the vessels) has been applied to fresh purpose. She took a year out of production to complete the commission. Drawing on the expertise developed over the previous twenty-five years, she has created a poetic evocation of her home county, and in its conception and manufacture has developed a much more literal iconography. In part this has been driven by her audiences: as she says, 'The public and the staff have welcomed the more accessible imagery.' She has found the challenge of the mural to be an opening to new possibilities: 'I do not accept that the Raku artist has to be "solipsistic" – the notion that the creative artist has to make *only* for himself is contemporary: navel contemplation can be stifling rather than inspirational.'

David Roberts

Clay is earth. This self-evident statement describes some potters better than others, but in particular it describes David Roberts. He lives and works in Yorkshire, and his work is centred like the granite outcrops that inspire him: it has the nuance of water-worn pebbles, where slight irregularities lead the eye on a tour that informs what the hands have felt. There is an evocation of archaeological time, where edges are worn and surfaces eroded. The making processes allude to the forces that created his landscape, capturing the spirit of the time-softened granite outcrops. He references

'use', while not making functional pots, and there is a sense of stripping away the superfluous:

> Over the years my ceramics have evolved from two elemental forms: a closed, containing shape derived from vessels for storage, and an open bowl shape derived from vessels for presentation ... There is a certain equivalence between the way that a path or trail moves across the local hills, and a tangential line exploring and defining the form of a pot.

The vessels are coiled to create contained 'interior space', a process that echoes the sedimentary deposition of silt in primordial seas; the pots are then built inexorably upwards, towards the sky. On Earth a period of erosion follows as the hills are sculpted by wind and rain, and there is a similar process at work in the creation of the skyline of Roberts' pots – the smooth hillsides of his forms are eaten away at the top, in the same way as are limestone pavements, to form the rims. Also, the pots decorated with the clay-resist technique seem to recreate the tracks left by the meandering of sheep across a hillside or the apparently endless line that a tractor describes as it carves into the land, pulling a plough.

One of the interesting aspects of David's work in the context of this book is that despite his avowed denial of Japanese influence in his work, there is nonetheless a very real feel of that tea-ceremony sensibility. There is a sense of commentary running through his work that continually touches on the dead world at the end of winter, a world of restraint, and of colour bleached from the land by an absence of sun. It is a ceramic practice built on restraint, both in the actual feel of the work and also, literally, in the holding back that occurs of the smoke by resists.

At the centre of his decorative practice lies a form of drawing utilizing resists: the first instance employs latex, the second a resist slip, and in the third example he creates a drawing by actually cutting through the resist slip.

The *latex resist* references the way that rock is worn away over the years by the wind and water, the extent of the wear dictated by how hard – or soft – the rock is. To achieve a surface of black on black Roberts first paints onto the leather-hard pot a burnishing slip made from the sieved clay body. The surface is burnished using pebbles or wood. Next, a contour pattern is applied with liquid latex. When this has dried the surface is gently wiped with a damp

Tile mural at Musgrove Park Hospital, Elizabeth Raeburn.

Two black vessels, David Roberts (above). *Vessel and pedestal, David Roberts.*

sponge. The dry latex protects the underlying burnished clay, and where the surface is exposed the clay is washed away, leaving slight ridges where the latex has protected the clay. The latex is peeled away before bisque firing, after which the pot is heated in a Raku kiln and smoked on top of a pile of sawdust, covered by a fibre-lined drum. The smoke penetrates the clay, and the burnished areas become a dark black; the washed and eroded surfaces are less shiny and appear greyer.

The second technique uses a *clay resist*: using a slip made from the sieved body clay, a series of contour lines is painted in negative onto the bisqued pot, which is fired in the Raku kiln and smoked on a pile of sawdust. The carbon penetrates a few millimetres into the surface. When the pot has cooled, it is washed and the raw clay resist can be scraped off, leaving the off-white colour of the clay against a series of smoke-blackened concentric dark lines. The surface is smoothed and polished with diamond pads.

The third type of resist is involved with the qualities, but not the presence of *glaze*; it creates an impression of drawing with a stick of charcoal, a crude but evocative line. The pot is burnished and bisque fired. It is then coated, by pouring, with a resist slip made from 50/50 silica and china clay. Over the top of this slip David Roberts sprays a glaze that will craze.

Glaze Recipe for Crazing

High alkaline frit	45
Borax frit	45
China clay	10

This recipe can be modified to give wide craze lines by increasing the proportion of borax frit, or a fine pattern by increasing the proportion of alkaline frit; through this surface David draws a graphic of lines. The pot is then Raku fired, and removed from the kiln to stimulate the crazing process; it is then smoked by standing on sawdust. The smoke penetrates the cracks in the glaze and also through the drawn lines, for by breaking the glaze the resist effect is destroyed: this allows the clay to be stained black while the resist areas remain the same colour as the body. The glaze and underlying slip are scraped off and the pot is washed: this leaves a bold drawing in lampblack against a fine network of black lines on the white clay ground.

Roland Summer

Trained in Austria as an architect, Roland Summer makes pots that reflect his researches into various low firing traditions of clay, in particular

*T*wo tall vessels, David Roberts.

*R*esist slip vase with black lines, Raku-fired, Roland Summer.

African, Pueblo Indian and Mediterranean pottery. His work concerns time and the atavistic nature of contemporary pottery – he looks back to a more sensate past and, with Messianic zeal, refers to 'the discovery of slowness'. He has deliberately chosen to employ the 'slow processes of coiling and burnishing', and wishes to emphasize the ironic place that the hand-made object has today: 'In a time of acceleration – that is, the speeding up of our culture (which is good to see in movies or computers) – it seems to be really anachronistic to spend so much time making a pot, and then to have to risk its perfection in the Raku firing. It takes more time to produce one pot than to produce one car!'

He also wants to emphasize the necessary place of the hand-made in our world where we are becoming increasingly detached from (tactile) contact with the physical world. Concerning a recent exhibition he says: 'I wanted to remove the card which dictated "Do not touch", because it is necessary for our culture still to feel things by hand, and *not* to give up this sense for a purely visual culture.'

He uses the 'resist slip method' of decorating some of his pots. The work is finished with a terra sigillata slip and then burnished; the vessels are coated with slip, and he cuts through it to leave a pattern on the terra sigillata slip below. When the pot is removed from its firing in the Raku kiln it is immediately quenched in water to make the glaze and slip peel off in order to reveal the marking on the clay surface.

The Raku technique is significant for Summer because it also embodies a quality of time; and although the firing is swift, it happens in real time: 'I like to have contact with the pot for the duration of the firing, and Raku allows me to have an influence on the creation of each piece. Also I like fire and the smell of smoke!'

Camille Virot

Camille Virot lives and works in Provence in the south of France. In both his work and in his mentality he pursues a course which, while it is very sophisticated, is also instinctive, reflecting the solid, coarse, brutish and inelegant side to the nature of clay. Edges are torn and surfaces eroded; they are often broken in this pursuit of the expression of the essential nature of clay and pot.

He portrays himself as a geologist (of the spirit of ceramics), searching for meaning in a minimal and direct form of expression. This he finds in Raku. Reflecting on his practice, dating from 1971, he says: 'Today I think that what interested me in Japanese Raku was not Japan, but that it could embody the spirit of Black Africa: an instinctive, physical and sacred work, that shows true respect for the material. The Japanese tea bowl is 'negre' in the sense that it is integrated with the natural scheme of things – it is not in competition with it.'

He does still make tea bowls (*see* page 15), and these are similar to, and have a relationship with, their Japanese predecessors. He also constructs work that is based much more strongly on his African experience, and acts to reject Western culture which he sees as expressive of 'domination' and 'exploitation'. Virot is engaged in a critique of Western artefacts which he sees as a continuation of the image of the Roman Empire which colours our two thousand years of culture, and is present in the grand architecture of his environment.

His artistic expression draws on Japanese and post-firing reduction Raku, combined with the bonfire-firing techniques employed by African potters. To Virot, Raku expression is a mélange of the deliberate, in the form of the Japanese tradition, and the spontaneous, as epitomized by African art. He echoes the sensibility of the tea masters by emphasizing a directness possible in Raku: 'Technique is not so important; the essential thing is to refine and intensify what you wish to express' (quoted in an article by F. de l 'Epine, in *Ceramics, Art and Perception* 25). And what he wishes to communicate is a partial geology, an archaeology and an architecture, the formation of rock, its analysis, the layerings of understanding and the building with his discoveries: 'I work within a set of themes: urns, agricultural machinery, geological boxes, the head and houses; and these pieces are produced alongside "conventional" tea bowls'. The geological boxes literally restate the qualities exhibited in geological cores taken from sampling the land.

Virot includes other materials in his work, too – these range from fired *ciment fondue*, to metal and shards of glass – all working together to create the impression of an ancient work. In order to effect these impressions Camille employs a minimum of devices. Thus he uses but one glaze – a white Borax glaze, and with this very minimal palette he is able to express a whole gamut of textures and surfaces – in shades of white. The range that he lists provides a good survey of glaze possibilities: 'Thin or

thick, more or less reduced in the firing, or afterwards; it can be little or well mixed, sifted or not, underfired, overfired, crackled, smoked, ground, pumiced, painted.'(F. de l'Epine in a catalogue essay.) The goal is to produce an object that speaks to us across cultures and apparent boundaries, seeking its realization in a magic conclusion fixed by fire.

*G*eological box, Raku-fired ceramic, Camille Virot.

Lidia Zavadsky

Lidia Zavadsky employs Raku as a referent to ancient ceramic practice. She throws on a potter's wheel to create pots of an heroic scale, deliberately selecting this technique as one superseded by industrial processes.The crazing of the glaze is used to suggest ageing, and also as a commentary on those many broken pots that visit us from the past, dug out of the ground and restored by the diligent work of conservators. In fact she started her career in Israel, repairing archaeological vessels – and these have a contemporary interest because they no longer retain their original purpose: their function is lost once they are broken. They enter a new, existential realm where they may be viewed in a different way – as objects of beauty; they have a story to tell, of lost civilizations. As a teacher she is exposed by the questioning of her students to issues concerning the contemporary role of ceramic objects in the late twentieth century, now that their functional requirements have ceased. Her current work parallels those restored pots – although the narrative is changed. She states that:

> The toxic glazes, while preventing functional use, invite a search for shapes detached from the vessel's expected utility, bringing about a quest for new combinations of forms and aesthetic meanings.

The oversized scale of the large Raku jars, which are 5ft (1.5m) tall, allude to the forms of earlier pots, which were made to be unbroken and functional. By changing the size of these pieces she is able to breathe new life into that aspect of a tradition that she might otherwise have believed was dead. Since the pots were too big to fire in one piece they were cut at the leather-hard stage, bisqued, and then Raku-fired in pieces; they were then reconstructed with glue and soft lead. Thus she has established a dialogue between pots from the past which were broken accidentally, and her contemporary work, which was designed to be broken from the outset. They are now installed in a permanent exhibition in the new Jerusalem municipality building, alongside vessels from authentic archaeological digs.

Archaeological jar, Raku-fired, height 5ft (1.5m), Lidia Zavadsky.

Contemporary Responses: The Metaphorical

Gail Bakutis

We are such stuff as dreams are made on, and
our little life is rounded with a sleep.

(*The Tempest*)

Gail Bakutis makes 'dream tablets', and this
work has developed out of a long, self-imposed
apprenticeship making vessel-based pieces, or
pieces influenced by architecture. These are both
areas where *form* plays a very significant part, but
to complement these architectonic pieces she
has developed a rich palette of Raku glazes that
are used with a flamboyance that reflects the culture of her Hawaiian home.

The Shakespeare quote seems most apposite
as Prospero the magician king is about to bid
farewell to his art on a spirit-inhabited island in
the sun: this is because Gail lives and works on
a tropical island, and her early training was in
the theatre. She became a theatre director fashioning realities out of dreams. Later, however,
she exchanged the drama of the stage for the dramatic glazes and performance of Raku.

'I'll break my staff, Bury it certain fathoms in
the earth, And deeper than did ever plummet
sound I'll drown my book.' At the end of *The Tempest* Prospero symbolically severs the connection
with his power; and in recent years Bakutis has
made a reappraisal of her life and work: she now
lives where land and rock is born, lava pouring
from the earth and solidifying in the sea as it
'freezes'. It is inchoate and formless, taking thousands of years till it is fashioned by the erosion
of wind, sea and plants into the forms that we
recognize as land. Dreams well up in our minds
and often have no apparent structure – there is a
darkness and an attempt to make sense of these
manifestations that come to us on the night.

Gail's work also has this aura about it. She
rolls large clay slabs that contain paper pulp as a
filler, to prevent cracking. These are fired stacked
on top of each other, or separated by plaster-
board (masonite); like this the air cannot penetrate to oxidize all of the cellulose, and carbon
stains mark the slabs in a series of mysterious

haloes. These interact with the ceramic
colourants, oxides, soluble salts and stains that
she has previously applied, and the qualities produced have the indefinite and shimmering surface seen in some of Rothko's paintings. Indeed
these pieces are designed for wall space, and they
do occupy that visually important place, once
the sole preserve of paintings and tapestries, and
now commandeered by the television.

In her work Gail allows the fire to paint,
directing the marks by judicious placement and
juxtaposition of materials, and reflecting her
home space: 'On the back of a volcano at the
edge of the sea.'

Dream tablet 'Vows', Gail Bakutis. (Photograph by Tibor Franyo.)

Joy Bosworth

Joy Bosworth has focussed on process and perception, in the way that things have been made, and the materials from which they have been created. These qualities were lost by the original makers and owners, and found by the roving eye of the artist. She is interested in the 'qualities of joining, forming and change in these discarded objects'.

Bottle forms, sawdust-fired with added gold leaf, Joy Bosworth.

Subsequent to this has come the ascription of value. Many people regard objects made from clay as without intrinsic value: which potter hasn't bemoaned their lot when faced by their disappointment in not achieving a good price for their work in the market place! To highlight this apparent discrepancy between low-status material and valuable finished object, Joy finishes her work, post-firing, by gilding the inside with 23-carat gold leaf. This provides a metaphor for an inner meaning, because in this way she returns value to her research source materials – found objects which '… by their surface show the history of the piece, i.e. old paintwork, rusty or patinated surfaces, burnt or broken objects … By collecting these objects I was giving them a value'. Bosworth cites a list of junk which serves as inspiration: 'Fast food and supermarket packaging, wet cardboard boxes, engine parts, ducting and exhaust pipes, burnt circuit boards, rusty buckets, tin cans, colanders, etc.' She recognizes the '*arte povera*' nature of the activity and, by emphasizing the reliance on 'detritus', she makes her own response to these findings all the more powerful, and contradictory.

Joy also emphasizes the contrast with artefacts found in major museums, which had an intrinsic value given by use. This resulted from their place as 'part of ceremonial life … or as vessels or tools which were part of everyday life'. In this one can find echoes of both the tea-ceremony philosophy and the new response to Raku brought by artists like Rick Hirsch in his investigations of abstracted ritual and ceremony, to make objects that offer a commentary on our own time.

She also links into another essential feature of the ceramic tradition, 'of clay vessels looking to artefacts made from other materials for their design inspiration, and usually being the poor man's version'. Thus she identifies cups, bottles and platters as the themes for reinterpretation; in the use of gold one also hears an echo of the gold and clay combination exploited by the Raku potters working for the tea ceremony. Those pots were also about damage and restoration, but whereas that Japanese work was a celebration of a rural aesthetic, what Joy is pursuing is a goal firmly fixed in the urban flotsam of the end of the twentieth century.

The final colour of the pieces is determined by the temperature of the bisque firing: the higher the bisque, the less carbon is absorbed from smoking in newspaper, and consequently the lighter the colour that the clay will be. Joy fires between 1060–1160°C in order to achieve this variation.

The gold leaf is an unfired adornment to the work. The area to be decorated in gold is prepared by coating with size; this is ready for gold leaf application when it is tacky, in about three hours. The gold is pressed onto the size by rubbing the protective paper backing hard with a stencil brush.

Rick Foris

The American potter Rick Foris makes dramatic work. His formative influence was potter John Natale, 'Whose work *always* knocked me out. Every time I'd see his work, at art fairs or galleries, it would evoke a "God, why didn't *I* think

Raku vessel, Rick Foris.

of that!" response. He generally made simple vessel shapes adorned with the most outrageous doodads – the pieces always looked so ceremonial. That did, and still does, interest and excite me.' Like many artists, Foris covers the traces of the sources for his influences, very carefully kicking dust in the face of anyone who enquires too closely into his motivation:

> I've always liked throwing, and my shapes tend to be pretty classical in nature. People are always asking me what my influences are – they think the pieces look Chinese, Egyptian, Mayan, and I think they're disappointed when I tell them 'none of the above'. I generally go into the studio with only my past pots as an influence and extrapolate from there. In fact, I try not to look at too much pottery for guidance as regards shape and style – I probably look at more architectural or natural shapes (seed pods, fruits and the like) for inspiration than anything else.

There is a powerful sense in his work of an artist creating his own ancient civilization, destroying what is there and presenting us with the artefacts that he has retrieved. There are no documents, and so an aura of mystery pervades the pieces. This absence of information extends even to those vessels that have an allusive hieroglyph pattern as a decoration in relief.

Foris was one of the potters whose work defined the nature of the fumed copper glaze; however, he grew increasingly frustrated by what he perceived were its limitations, and the straitjacket that seemed to be placed around him through his association with a technique. This was an interesting dilemma, because it actually provided much of what he wanted aesthetically. It wasn't, though, a fundamental and integral artistic and philosophical necessity like Rick Hirsch's relationship to the surface; rather it was a technique that, increasingly, failed to deliver the goods:

> After working with the copper matt glaze for ten years or so, my surfaces shifted more and more to the use of acrylics for their colour ... copper matt had turned into a monster. By the mid-80s, the copper matt surfaces were becoming a cliche.

Many potters have been seduced by the superficial 'flashiness' of Raku, only to reject this surface value as their vision of the work that they wish to make becomes clearer in their mind.

Rick has taken elements of this rich vocabulary, both crackles and lustre, and supplemented it with post-firing painting with non-fired acrylics.

Susan and Steven Kemenyffy

Susan and Steven Kemenyffy make 'archetypal art', his work seeming to define the masculine, hers the feminine. They make truly collaborative work in adjacent studios – it is a celebration of difference in unity, where the whole is certainly more than the sum of its parts. The pieces that Steven transfers to Susan to decorate speak of energy, where clay has been slapped, pummelled and forced to perform. This is an heroic endeavour, with clay and the artist under test. These vigorous and vital forms and gouged surfaces are then considered anew as blank canvasses by his wife:

> First comes the clay, formed as Steven so desires; then comes direct drawing (always from a model) with India ink on the wet clay, never on paper beforehand.

As the pieces are fired vertically, incised lines are necessary to keep the glaze from running.

> The incisions also serve as reminders that my contribution to the finished result of this flamboyant process is as one team member to the whole ... My images are not decorations, which in the history of art is a word often used in a perjorative sense, as art without meaning, content or importance: they are observations and remarks about the people and events which constitute our personal life as it has been and is lived, at the end of this millennium ... I have been exposed to the whole history of art since the creation, and find inspiration in all the best and the finest objects and images that have managed to survive. A Kemenyffy Raku seeks to embody the silence of a Vermeer; the flowing powerful lines inscribed in Michaelangelo's drawing of a Sybil; an inherent sense of place within the gently rolling hills of an American Pennsylvania; a personal and professional working relationship with another artist, whose own idiosyncratic perceptions and abilities add to the mystery.

Underneath these immediate appearances it is possible to identify their opposites. His anima shows through in the care and attention to firing; hers, in

*'T*he Ghaffari Commission'; work in progress, Steven and Susan Kemenyffy. (Photograph by J.L. Color, Erie PA.)

*'T*he Ghaffari Commission', Raku-fired (below). (Photograph by MMG Photography.)

Installation of mural, Steven and Susan Kemenyffy.

Slip cast ceramic form, Raku-fired, Mike Marshall.

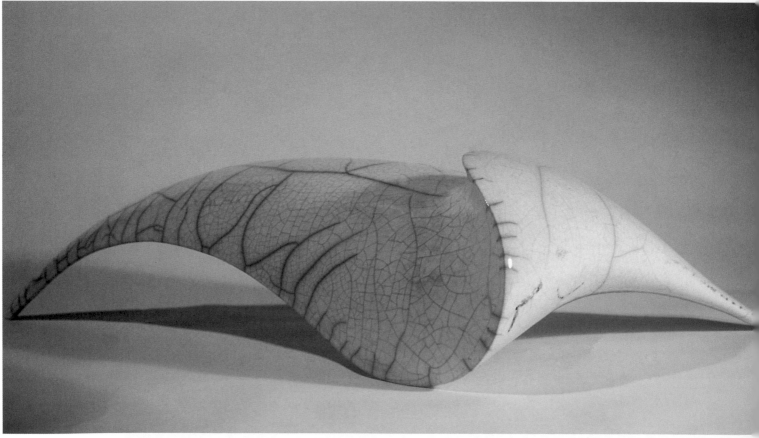

the form of respect for Michaelangelo, infuses all her work – in its pursuit of the 'curving and elliptical' line she is seeking for a 'shared sensuousity' that is exhibited in much great, hieratic art.

One can see why the Raku process is attractive to them, with its 'remarkable palette of subtle and brilliant colour. We are at the height of our incredibly vibrant North American autumn. Brilliant scarlet leaves clothe oak and sweetgum, before rotating in the chilling air, to push away paths of summer green. The textured, golden world can so easily become a state of mind.'

Theirs is a Raku of muscular form underpinning painting in a unique combination. Intense colour battles and then unifies with forms fashioned on an epic scale from coarse clay. Swathes of lustre add to the feeling of heightened sensibility, making for a drama of Wagnerian proportions.

Mike Marshall

Mike Marshall's work demonstrates all the contradictions possible in Raku-fired clay. His pieces generate a feeling of lightness and airi-

ness, each one balancing on acutely angled wings. The ideas are influenced by the sea: the skimming of pebbles across its surface and the streamlining of the great oceanic mammals. The work is slip-cast, using a body that partly vitrifies at Raku firing temperatures; consequently severe cracking of the clay is always a possibility, and extreme care must be exercised when heating and cooling it.

The pieces are first created in plaster of Paris, and then cast in a mould; this permits great precision and finely articulated edges. The crackle glaze breaks over these, which helps to emphasize the delicacy of the medium.

Mari Oda

Mari was born of Japanese parents in Papua New Guinea and has had quite an international education, culminating in a Master of Arts programme in England. Despite all these changes in her environment, her work is ineluctably Japanese in inspiration and execution. She cites the influence of Zen – not the ceramic creations that were the precursors of Raku today, but the formal *Zen garden, Kyoto.*

*'Barefoot walk',
Mari Oda.*

gardens of raked gravel and disposed boulders that are such a notable presence in some Buddhist temples in Kyoto. In these very deliberate arrangements the designers attempted, by allusion, to recapture a significant experience of the natural world within the restricted space of the temple grounds:

> My work is influenced by the traditional Japanese concept of worshipping nature. Many of the stone gardens in Japan deal with the idea of recreating nature and providing a contemplative situation in which one could purify one's spirit.

Mari's ceramics have the quality of large, water-worn rocks, yet they also suggest the softness that just invites you to nestle into it, in contrast to the hardness of the clay: this is accentuated by smoothing the bare fired surface with diamond pads. Other pieces are concerned with crumpling, and the folds found in the human body (*see* page 89). She chooses sawdust-firing as a means of processing, and this results in a warm clay and a rich black that emphasizes the enveloping sensuousness of her pieces:

> It is a natural and potent black that penetrates the surface of the clay. I attempt to fire the forms so that the surfaces acquire sheen in the blackness, and I polish some of the work to achieve extra shine. The darkness of the surface retains energy and depth, and is reminiscent of the japanning seen on many tablewares in Japan: this black lacquered effect is commonly used on everyday and ceremonial wares, and is, to me, symbolic of the Japanese tradition.

The distorting mirror of her eye imagines the human body echoing fruits and rocks, and discovers traces of the natural world in the bends and folds of the flesh; thus her work deals with the seductive physicality of clay. The pieces range from those that can be held in the arms, to objects on a grander scale, such as seats. There is in this work a hint of Claes Oldenberg, particularly in the sense of contrast as she makes these apparently soft objects hard. Some of these large pieces have been vitrified and exhibited floating on water – and this creates another conceptual dilemma: the buoyant rock. Mari might be described as 'An artist of the floating world' – and like Ichiguro, her work has that measured poise, but controlled passion, sitting elegantly as it does between England and Japan.

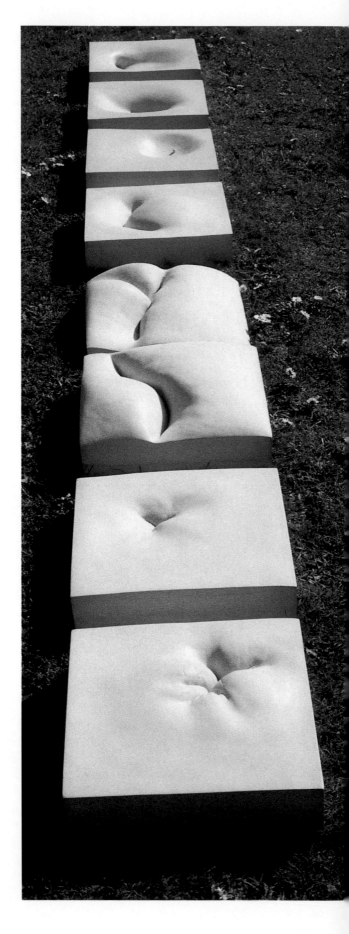

Magdalene Odundo

Magdalene Odundo's work is concerned with void and form: it contains trapped space and also occupies space. She says: 'The work is to dare: it is to question ideas and thoughts that arise through the tactile' – and as such it owes far more to Brancusi than to a fascination with fire. And indeed this interest in flame doesn't seem to exist, because she states unequivocally: 'I hate firings!' Like Picasso and Modigliani, Odundo looks to art from the African continent – but more than this, she is reclaiming her heritage from the West by examining the way in which these artists have synthesized that material. 'I love antiquities, pre-glaze and pre-competition; I see the universal values embodied in the undifferentiated and geometric forms of the early ceramics – the idea of capturing poetry and enclosing it in these pieces. Then the work develops like the improvisation of Miles Davis in jazz.'

Her work references a complex of ideas: it looks to the figures of pregnant women, and to cicatrization, the scarification used to decorate the skin in patterns of raised weals; it is influenced by objects ranging from traditional archaic pots to modernist sculpture; and in the final analysis it represents the ultimate expression of a potter's desire to control surface, while using the qualities of low-temperature firing. It also highlights the sophistication attainable in so-called alternative firings, and raises the issue of what constitutes 'the primitive'.

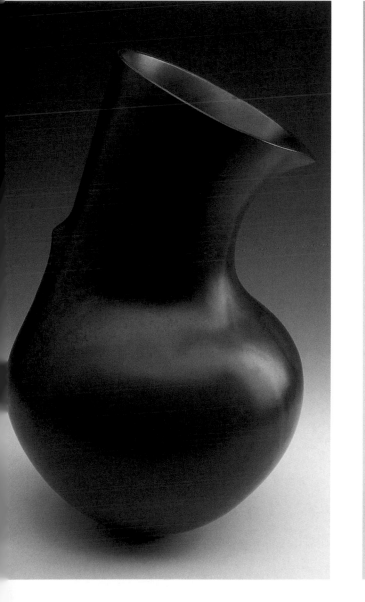

*C*oiled vessel with *burnished* terra sigillata, *Magdalene Odundo* (bottom left).

*C*oiled vessel with *burnished* terra sigillata, *Magdalene Odundo*. *(Photograph by P. van de Kruis.)*

The critical, modernist overview of African art – a tradition in which Magdalene Odundo seems to have such a significant contemporary part to play – is largely Western, since the explorers, ethnographers, historians, archaeologists and artists who supposedly 'discovered' African art came from Europe and latterly from America. In much of the earlier writing there is the sense of the 'Heart of Darkness' that Conrad wrote of – an energy and an unknowability, our shadow. As a Kenyan, Odundo has a clear, critical perspective of the culture of the continent: 'African art was constantly permeating Western culture but none of the research was being returned to the African continent.'

She also has a clear view of the post-colonial heritage, recognizing this as a significant problem deriving from non-ownership of that cultural capital. Part of this is due to the convenient narrative of 'bonfire firings' which most potters in the West know from the writings of Michael Cardew, and from Hal Riegger's inspirational book, *Primitive Pottery*. There is a sense of the 'primitive' being in some way less sophisticated than the Japanese/Bauhaus heritage and thereby closer to the natural: however, Magdalene's work is a complex disavowal of this assumption.

She is at pains to relate her own artistic and ceramic experiences not just to 'the African' – after all, the name of a whole continent – and in fact not even specifically to 'the Kenyan', where indeed she was born, but very precisely to the home of her forebears: the Abaluhyia nation. She also wishes to make it quite clear that her work does not so much focus on the utilitarian tradition, but on court ceramics; the latter pieces exist in archaeology, and not in ethnographic collections. She places her work amongst the objects which did not belong to the everyday – but nevertheless she wants to maintain that her work is functional, insofar as aesthetic need is actually answering an imperative of use: 'In Africa, functionality never has a one-dimensional character. An object could be used in a ceremony for the dead, for instance, and then be given to the king for safe-keeping and prosperity. Those different meanings are preserved in the object. They become part of its history.' (*Ceramic Histories*, by Marla Burns.)

Magdalene Odundo's work commands respect across the world. Despite this she is aware that the labelling that derives from the apparent way in which the work is made can still constitute a ghetto: she says: 'I am not trying to disassociate myself from Africa and pottery – I am dealing with the universality of ceramics, and my intention is to celebrate clay beyond the narrow confines of a pigeon-hole … In my own education, African pots were, sadly, not prioritized; the emphasis was on European art.'

Magdalene Odundo's work is burnished with a terra sigillata, and exquisitely finished with a firing that impregnates the clay with carbon. The clay contains iron, which produces a lustre on cooling (a discovery she made in her post-graduate researches, recapitulating the ancient knowledge of generations of long-deceased potters). Despite the warmth and humanity of these pieces, she partially disavows the ceramic heritage, looking instead to twentieth-century art as her initial inspiration. She says that the desire for the severe black finish to the pots comes not from a fascination with fire, but because she is interested in the effects of a monochrome finish to emphasize the form of the pot. The work is fired in a saggar in a gas kiln packed with sawdust. The pots are coiled, and although she claims to enjoy the process, it has no significance in itself: rather she sees this merely as a means to an end.

Robert Piepenburg

Robert Piepenburg came to Raku in the 1960s and still carries with him much of the transcendental philosophy that he embraced with the discovery of the medium. His work aspires to an evocation of other-worldliness, of altars and sacrificial tables, and there is an aura of entering consecrated ground when one examines his Raku thinking. This is in strong contrast to many of the younger protagonists who state that the process is just one amongst the many that they could have chosen. However, as a writer of one of the early books on the medium, Piepenburg has had an opportunity to reflect on Raku practice over three decades:

As I see it, Raku is a complex phenomenon in the world of ceramics. Like a multicolored jewel, it reflects Eastern philosophy and tradition, yet it is strikingly contemporary and episodic as a means of artistic expression. But even these timeless and mysterious qualities rely on the firing process for buoyancy. For many Rakuists the act of firing becomes the very thrill and substance of the work, while for others it takes on some inspirational or spiritual sense, and becomes a uniquely personal and creatively liberating way to work

with clay. After thirty years as a Rakuist I am still drawn to the sacred moments surrounding the firing process; but more than any one thing, I find a comforting influence in the transcending qualities it brings to the surfaces of my work. Raku has always edited my clay work, and by refusing to be a successful medium for functional, utilitarian ware, it has disarmingly initiated a more sculptural or aesthetic direction for me to explore. Today I celebrate those influences, not simply for cultivating my sculptural sensitivities or for its rewarding surface sensations, but more profoundly, for touching my creative spirit.

Raku-fired slab, Robert Piepenburg.

Raku-fired slabs drilled and bolted to rusted steel, Gail Piepenburg.

Tim Proud

Tim Proud describes his work as 'deliberately abstract', and he is overtly fascinated by ambiguity and duality: 'It is my aim to weld two separate and equal ideas, landmarks as navigational aids through spatial territory, and landmarks as cultural icons within the land.' This is a combination of spiritual and practical functions that recalls the intentions of the Zen tea masters. As a result of the change in use of clay over the centuries, Tim has a different interpretation for the

*R*aku-fired, Tim
Proud.

context of his work, closely following the lead of Ruskin, Morris and Leach in seeking meaning in the activity of work, and in the medium of clay itself. A Zen monk would look to the Raku-fired tea bowl as being part of a ritual activity forcing the drinker to focus on the here and now; Proud's spiritual interests make him take a more pragmatic yet secular view than the Japanese. He identifies a quality in contemporary craftwork that points to an intrinsic value in the object itself: 'Its worth is measured not only in terms of time, materials, beauty and permanency, but equally by its own inherent power to evoke a response and stir passions.'

This focus on the material is a very significant attitude in terms of our understanding of Raku at the millennium. As makers we have a belief in the power of hand-made objects to inspire, and Tim's explication is that: 'What interests me is the sense of their being objects that we treasure, that and their association with places or people.' This manifests itself in the way that he interprets his own work, the artefacts referring to actual objects in the environment. Thus an exhibition of his ceramics suggests spires, hilltop beacons and great towers – there is no sign of the individuals that made them; they are stark and uninhabited, and he sees them merely as '... reliquary ideas, as points of contact for our thoughts and feelings'.

By questioning him about the Raku-fired forms, one can gain an insight into his motivations, and the symbolism and references implicit in them: 'Compositionally the spires of my boxes are separate pieces which penetrate the box form in such a way as to point up and down, marking as it were the exact point on the ground where the piece stands, straddling a fixed point or meridian line.' This fixes the vertical co-ordinates of the piece. The horizon is indicated by the slabs slotted through the pyramidal spire, and this horizontal eye-line is a centring device, which stands for the 'world's horizon'. In a world of shifting values and no ultimate reality (in the sense spoken of by the great religions), we can perceive in modern craftwork an attempt to reach some of the verities that were the sole domain of the sacred in a previous age.

Tim suggests that the use of lustre indicates the '... sense of wealth and value, like the gold leafing of a letter', and he uses the light-gathering qualities of gold and silver to stand for spiritual values by 'enhancing light'. He also employs a variety of glaze techniques: 'Glazes are brushed over textured surfaces to pick up and maximize the contrast of marks and piercing employed in the body of the pieces. Points and tips of the pyramids, previously burnished at the making stage, are dipped to give a richer and more fluid quality, creating a dynamic focus.'

The Raku process works perfectly as a medium for an artist trying to answer some of these questions. The inbuilt appearance of age and preciousness, brought about through a use of lustre, changes what might just appear to be a pretty decorative effect into something more profound.

Peder Rasmussen

If the Danish potter Peder Rasmussen uses a technique, it is because it will give him the qualities and the surface that he wants for his work – it is not the kind of fascination, even obsession, with technique that may be identified in a number of other potters. So, rather than embracing a certain method and spending a long time investigating its possibilities, he seems to know intuitively what he wants, and his way is then to search out a technique to accomplish it. This is why he ceased working in stoneware and devoted himself to Raku for about ten years. He relates his inspiration for his Raku to a desire to express a range of feelings about his natural environment in Denmark: 'The reason I started working with Raku was a sense of longing for heavier textures than it seemed I could satisfactorily find in stoneware. Raku offered me a fresh, natural (nature-like) possibility in the potential colours of the glazes.'

He uses soluble salts in a post-firing treatment: 'I saw a Soldner show, and I asked Aage Birck, who was there too, what this guy did with his surfaces – and Aage said: "It's easy ... iron chloride. You spray it on while the pot is still hot. You take it out of the kiln at 1000°C and spray it." He could have told me of course, that this is the best way you get rid of competitors (it is as poisonous as hell), but he didn't!'

The work concerns somatic forms. Peder felt that Raku, with its more intimate relationship and involvement in the firing process, would better convey his message – an attempt to capture 'hills and lakes and woods, soft and not too big'.

Currently he is firing brightly coloured glazes at earthenware temperatures, without any secondary reduction or post-firing treatments. In order to reach this stage, which is like Raku without reduction (and hence the muting of colours), he has spent a long time playing with Raku.

*'S*imple pot, vase with black cuts', Peder Rasmussen.

Rick Rudd

Rick Rudd is a potter working in New Zealand who has also ostensibly ceased using Raku firing processes in his work; yet in fact he retains many of the features and qualities commonly associated with the practice: 'For me, Raku firing was a process rather than an aesthetic idea.' His work exhibits a preoccupation with line and form, and he used Raku glaze and firing to emphasize

this; but '… after so many years of the process I yearned for a type of firing which did not include a dirty and smoky environment'. He adds: 'I stopped Raku firing because I wanted my work to change.'

While working with Raku he focussed closely on the classic repertoire of white crackle glaze contrasting with black carbon-impregnated body, and this monochrome palette is one that remains dominant in his current output. (A survey of the

work of other Raku potters in the late 1970s and 1980s sees a number of other clay artists with the same concerns; Dave Roberts and Martin Smith both used these qualities almost to the exclusion of all other Raku qualities.)

His statements reveal no sentimental attachment to the social activity of Raku, and he denies that his 'approach to Raku firing had anything to do with that of the Japanese aesthetic or with American Abstract Expressionism'. There is an ascetic approach in his words to the activities taking place that is the antithesis of the hedonistic bravado of many 'party-style' firings; it also sets a precedent for a ceramic practice where Raku is just a technique that provides a set of qualities and nothing else – and if one adopts this attitude it is certainly not possible to use Raku as the basis for a philosophy of clay, fire and action. Indeed, it exemplifies the extreme position of the potter who chooses Raku just for the quality of the surfaces that it provides.

*R*aku bowl, Rick Rudd.(Photograph by Richard Wotton.)

*M*ultifired bowl, Rick Rudd (left). (Photograph by Richard Wotton.)

The pieces themselves were controlled, and the black was controlled. With experience and with time I learned how to control the crackle, and within reason I could decide where I wanted the crackled areas. By removing the work from the kiln and submerging it in woodshavings as quickly as possible I could achieve a good black on fairly thin pieces. To achieve a crackle on the glazed areas, after a few minutes of smoking I would either uncover or feel my way around in the woodshavings and rub the glazed area to cool it with a Kevlar mitten. Then I resubmerged the piece in woodshavings and in this way I could 'place' the crackle to a large extent. ['Kevlar' is a synthetic material with heat-resistant properties.]

Despite this avowed denial of many of the tenets of Raku philosophy, the demands of firing the work and of getting the precise effects that he desired, led him to '… remove pieces from the kiln using lined Kevlar mittens'. For many potters, this entering into an intimate relationship with the kiln is turned into a sacramental ritual – but for Rudd and others it is no more than a process necessary to achieve the outcomes required for the work. Interestingly, Rick's most recent work develops the theme of matt clay read against seductive glaze along the lines pursued by many contemporary Raku artists. What he gets from adopting a new firing procedure is a harder clay body and the ability to work comfortably at a much larger scale. Thus through denying, and finally rejecting, current Raku practice, Rick Rudd actually creates work that echoes that call for restraint uttered by Zen monks centuries ago.

*'Standing forms',
Antonia Salmon.*

Antonia Salmon

Antonia Salmon makes pots that appear to deny themselves – her work is a fashioning of dreams and of the spaces in between: we know that the material is clay, yet the evocation is of the ethereal. The clay is dense and yet appears almost translucent – the surface seems to shimmer as the light reflects from it.

To begin with the pots are thrown on the wheel, but these are then cut and joined to create a variety of simple volumes, and a variety of spaces between. The surfaces are refined by scraping with sharp, hard tools: 'Burnishing three or four times as the clay dries out allows me to get to know the work intimately.' This procedure may seem to share a certain resonance with Neolithic hand axes, though Antonia denies this; and certainly when she describes her work she does not use the language of those instruments of death and sacrifice, but the tones of a solicitous creator:

> By the time each piece is finished and dry I feel a kind of detached care, because I have given it of my best. After bisque firing I feel the work looks lifeless, but the smoke firing breathes new life into it, an uncontrollable and sometimes destructive energy … After the quiet care of the workshop, submitting the work to the smoke firing represents a letting go, a precariousness and a danger. In retrieving the work from the ashes I can welcome some pieces to the world, assess which others need refiring – many are fired four or five times – and break up the 'no hopers'.

So there *is* a cruelty here, in the selecting and editing, and the symbolic value of firing and life, rebirth and death *is* found in her special relationship to the process. This is not the bravado and hubris of the Raku firers, with their roaring kilns, but a deeply contemplative approach to making. Her work is as much about an attitude of mind as it is about forms found in nature: it is a focussed introspection, using its own attentiveness as a subject.

The Zen quality of *wabi* can be identified in Antonia's pieces, although as a potter she does not feel that she has been directly influenced by Japanese thought or ceramic tradition. Nevertheless, it shows that it can still be a relevant attitude of mind, and it is an important concept in appreciating work which is intended as an object of contemplation: 'I am attempting to express a sense of tension and also centredness within one abstract form … a work poised in space.'

She hopes for a genuine gut reaction to her clay creations, an appreciation from the heart: 'I desire the finished work to lift away from personal input, to cut through verbal interpretation and to speak directly, at a gut level, to the onlooker.'

One of the parameters that Antonia Salmon frequently changes is the firing medium: 'I'm always experimenting with different wood types and quality of sawdust.' In this way she controls the degree of reduction and the blackening of the clay, and also the way that the carbonization is burnt away to give whites and greys: fine resinous sawdust gives the darkest blacks, hardwood shavings and newspaper the lightest coloration.

Kate Schuricht

Kate Schuricht makes severe slip-cast cylinders, and then softens these qualities with voluptuous Raku glazes. She quotes Jun'ichiro Tanazaki:

> We do love things that bear the marks of grime, soot and weather, and we love the colours and sheen that call to mind the past that made them. Living among these objects is in some mysterious way a source of peace and repose.
> (From *In Search of Shadows*.)

Kate analyses her work in terms of the precepts of traditional Japanese Raku, whilst at the same time working in a modern and minimalist tradition; so although the process that she

Raku-fired vases, Kate Schuricht.

employs to make the pieces is quite alien to the organic nature of tea ceremony, she feels that her work embodies the spirit of that philosophy, as well as the energy of contemporary practice:

> Slip-casting the forms lends a certain detachment to the work, and because I purposely avoid indulging in any creativity and expression in this stage of the making process, I have much greater freedom when it comes to applying and using glaze. With a simple form, I work at this point with the quality of the glazes, part-covering the forms, layering and wrapping them as though they were thin fabrics, each layering revealing something of the level below. The relationship is between the hidden and the revealed … In groups the pieces become like carefully placed fragments of the landscape, abstracted elements of water, horizons, rock, all interlinking and flowing from one to another … although silent and still, they speak of the fire and heat, the smoke and flames of Raku.

'Line and displacement VI' 1992. Carbonized 'T' material, aluminium leaf, slate 12 × 11 × 14in (31 × 28 × 36cm), Martin Smith.

Martin Smith

Martin Smith has featured in many discussions on Raku, but, like other contemporary artists, he denies any influence from the Japanese tradition: 'It was just a technique that I tried as an undergraduate.' Indeed much of his present work is not recognizable within the normal parameters that categorize Raku or sawdust firing. His is not an obsession with smoke and randomness, but a conceptual and mathematical investigation into form and surface. Nevertheless it is still possible to identify some traces of Raku's importance in Smith's development as an artist. He states that Raku was just another way to fire clay, but it provided him with a tractable language through which to articulate his concerns. For his postgraduate degree he did some of the earliest research in England into the new and already popular technique of post-firing reduction, and the significance to later Raku development in this type of work was that it exhibited an exceptionally high degree of control in the firing of a graphic pattern of glaze applied using resists composed of masking tape.

'Control' is a preoccupation in all his work – yet within these self-imposed strictures he permits varying glimpses of imprecision, notably in the mark-making and texture; he just determines certain areas to be smooth, rough or lustrous. In sub-atomic physics Heisenberg's uncertainty principle states that at any given time it is impossible to give the exact coordinates of an electron – and Martin gives the same degree of freedom to his clay work. Thus there is a sub-text in his work where imprecisions arise, and these random qualities are significant in that they provide a foil to his passion for sharp and perfectly articulated surface. In the early pieces it was via his work with a white crazing glaze: the crackle glaze was extremely accurately applied, because he could control how wide or narrow the crackle was by selective cooling of the hot glaze with wet cloth – but the resulting patterns were not totally predictable.

He is like the kestrel with its aloof and unremitting gaze, and its ultimately unsentimental dissection of its prey: he presents clay, and the concept of 'the pot', as material for analysis. So why is his work seductive? One aspect is the extreme novelty of having the nature of clay and its methodologies examined and interrogated with the mind of an architect or engineer, rather than the caressing touch of what Cardew referred to as a 'mud and water

man'. Smith is interested in the skin of a clay object and the way that it covers, describes and articulates both the inside and the outside of a form: the interior volumes meet rims, and then the eye is carried to the outside, which has been finished with a machined precision. In his new work he uses a red clay body, contrasting the 'poverty' of 'flowerpot clay' with the lushness of gold and platinum leaf which is applied after the firing; thus in this work he is able to comment on the distinction that Cardew makes between 'town (or court) potters' and 'country potters'. There is also the feeling that he can comment on past cultures and civilizations, for ceramic is the material that relates to those early histories, persisting in the ground long after the other traces have rotted away.

Despite these concerns, it is possible to identify a set of preoccupations that certainly recall the demands of the tea masters. There is the interest in the nature of the undulating rim, and the way that it leads our eye around the form and into its interior, and then to the relationship of the inner wall to the outer. The handling quality of the surface is of paramount importance, although obviously at a distant remove from a tea bowl. This is an extreme vision, but one that derives some of its humanity through association with Raku and sawdust.

Some of Martin's work achieves a profound black due to the penetration of carbon from sawdust firing; this visually isolates the form as a black object. There are the vestiges of post-reduction treatments with sawdust or perlite actually incorporated into the clay body to give a randomized texture as it burns out in the firing. It is significant in the Raku context that after firing, perlite needs to be washed out from the pores in the clay: this echoes post-reduction quenching in water and the washing off of built-up carbon from the process of secondary reduction. The work on the vessel does not end with its washing off after its removal from the kiln: the surface is then smoothed and polished with grinding wheels and diamond pads, and the various parts are finally assembled.

Contemporary Responses: The Representational

Roy Ashmore

'We are a part of, and not apart from, the land on which we walk.' This American Indian sentiment informs the ceramic sculpture of Roy Ashmore, who describes his work as 'landscapes in a figure'. As in many examples of contemporary craft, his work not only references landscape and the figure, but also the physical forces and processes that actually fashioned them – it is not merely about the forms that are found in nature, but it concerns the finding of analogues for sedimentary deposition and forms of erosion. The former is achieved by actually incorporating dug, unprocessed clay, and sheets of broken slate (clay that has been transformed geologically by pressure and heat). Observing the charring effect given by secondary reduction in Raku and sawdust firing showed him how he wished to finish the work; and it was then but a short step to incorporate combustibles actually within the clay. Also the use of materials found locally – grass, twigs and so on – means that the artist can make the work relate to a particular environment.

The form is created by pressing a conglomerate of clay and fillers, such as grass and paper

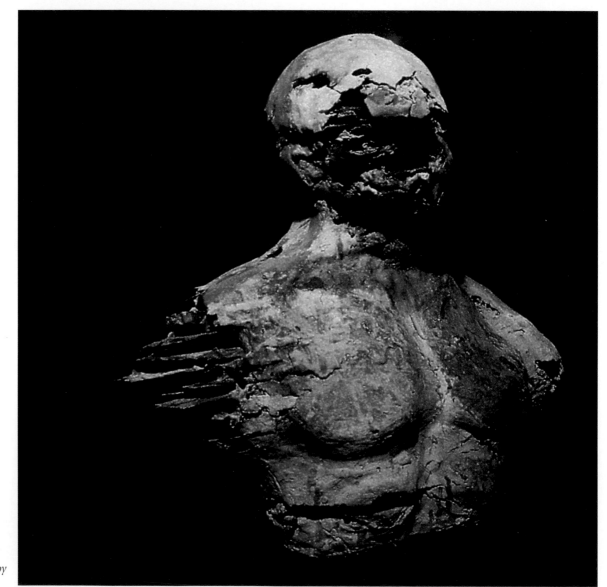

'The cycle', clay and slate, sawdust-fired, Roy Ashmore.

pulp, into a plaster mould. As these materials burn out, the illusion of erosion commences. This is a process that can be continued physically after firing, as the ceramic is left quite soft by firing at low temperatures. This burning out of combustibles can allude to natural processes and allow chance elements to enter the complex aesthetic formula, as the specific way in which the materials burn out cannot be controlled. This burning away from within is the only presence of air in the pieces, as they are built solid; they are not containers in any conventional sense, but function as metaphoric vessels.

Ian Byers

Ian Byers' book *Raku* was published in 1990, and for him it was a significant step in the medium. The written word played an important part in the construction of his own philosophy of making, too, particularly the books of Nigrosh and Hirsch: their visual content suggested 'energy and involvement'. He also remembers '… a book on Nigerian pots, published with Michael Cardew's involvement. This book immediately engaged me with the beauty of bare surfaces, sculptural modelling and surface texture, with all the nuances of detail, immediacy of touch and nakedness as a quality to be explored.'

Here he pulls together a number of important strands in the development of Raku. There is a confluence of the Japanese Raku aesthetic and the low-firing methodologies rediscovered in African and South American pottery traditions. Also in his work there are echoes of a much more primitivist and deliberately crude handling of clay. The colour is applied in broad, bold expressive streaks; the clay is simply and brusquely handled. All is informed by a meditation on the word 'Raku':

> The sixteenth century in Japan was a sort of Renaissance for Japanese arts and crafts, with many people trying new things. When I think of the word 'Raku' it creates images in my mind of those first steps in making and designing using the technique. The essence of those thoughts is rooted in the fact of it being unknown territory to all involved, and the fact that the ability to make work in this way was available not just to potters but to anyone who was interested. The resonance for me therefore is with the unknown and discovery.

Stephen Charnock

Stephen Charnock creates archaeology. He makes objects that apparently carry an already archaic knowledge, and he digs for information, found not merely in clay and those physical artefacts from the past, but also embedded within language and the land. His family farm in Northern England, where he has heard the local colloquial speech; as a student his tutorials sometimes became investigations in etymology (the source and meaning of words). This probing into his familial past enabled Steve to personalize his work – what became interesting to him was his growing realization that both he and his father had a relationship to the land. Steve itemizes a set of responses that would not have sounded out of place in the poetical melancholy of seventeenth-

Horse and rider box, Raku-fired, Ian Byers.

'*B*oggard', found
clay and locally sourced
sherds; sawdust-fired,
Stephen Charnock.

'*B*oggard', found
clay and locally sourced
sherds; sawdust-fired,
Stephen Charnock.

century Japan: 'The colour of the earth, disintegrating buildings, ploughed furrows and the scorched marks left on fields by burnt stubble all carry a particular emotional intensity.' (*See* the photograph 'Burnt wood' page 81.)

The farmer views the land not just for what it produces, but also in terms of a mythic entity: he is a guardian of the past for the future who will one day inherit the ground that he ploughs today. What Steve does in his work is to deal with the land in a conceptual way and search for meaning within the material itself; he also creates for a future:

> Marks left by past civilizations beg to be pondered and interpreted. Archaeologists scrape away layers of earth to reveal fragments of the past. Like the pages of a book, the earth preserves the tangible record of mankind's progress within its depth. This 'book' is difficult to decipher, and its language is ambiguous yet mysteriously universal, reminding us all of the transient nature of life.

The 'Boggard' series was stimulated into being by a confluence of Raku and other burning processes, clay collage and assemblage and the dredging up of the ancient, northern word for

spook, spectre, or indeed the devil! It is the sense of an essentially unknowable spiritual power pushing from behind. He not only took the name from home, but also the clay from the fields. The objects then enter the public domain and are open to interpretation.

> As human beings we give form and meaning to objects. They become vehicles which convey emotion and social history. Through time, the meaning of such objects is lost; they instead become symbols. We are intimately connected with such objects, and yet, paradoxically, they maintain their aloofness because they are inanimate.

These images are constructed in a body cast. They are reminiscent of the art of ancient civilizations and composed from the ceramic detritus of our own very recent past – in Steve's case shards dug from his own familiar land; a place where he now has his workshop.

> I can best describe my work as a personal archaeology, a search for relics within myself. Clay has become an essential medium through which I can interpret my finds, and in so doing give meaning to my life.

Michael Flynn

Michael Flynn believes that one of the functions of art is to open up, in the viewer's sensibility, doors that have become closed and ways of thinking that have become ossified. He is quite adamant that 'Interpretation must be open'. He relates the story of his own intensely Catholic upbringing, thus implying that one of the possible interpretations of his work is a 'cultural east of Europe, and it may be a reference to the care required when talking in such repressive political environments. These are complex pieces that work on a number of different levels, and which employ a sophisticated attitude to firing that gives nuance to Flynn's dramas.

The building techniques that he employs have developed 'from modelling the pieces solid, and hollowing out, to pinching the forms out with an ever thinner wall [which] … converted the

'A word in the ear', Raku-fired, Michael Flynn.

response from five hundred years ago'. This might be appropriate for the piece entitled 'A word in the ear', as one of the explanations for the Immaculate Conception was that the Holy Spirit entered through Mary's ear; or perhaps Jesus' betrayal by Judas is suggested. On the other hand, following on from this observation, much of his present work is done in the formerly communist arbitrariness of hollowing out an ostensibly finished piece into an act which was an integral part of the process of creating the piece'.

Raku allows a different relationship, with the clay, to conventional firing techniques. Flynn first studied painting, and was searching for a ceramic equivalent to quick sketching and painting. Most pottery techniques involve a long interval in between the different phases of making, drying and firing, whereas the open Raku clays dry quickly and can be fired rapidly – a Raku piece can be finished in the time it takes to finish a painting. As it is not necessary to fire to a precise temperature the firings can vary dramatically, so that a dripping, runny glaze is achieved by overfiring a piece, or a dry, underfired surface by removing the piece early from the kiln.

Raku provides a vocabulary that is rich in nuance:

> Metal lustres, the blackened clay, the fat crackly whites … and the expressive possibilities of the raw, cracked surfaces and dripping or globular glazes … With experience the practitioner can very closely determine where a glaze might run or drip, or where the focus of attention might be drawn to the weight and balance in terms of chiaroscuro, and so on.

Sue Halls

Sue Halls' work derives from observation and abstraction. Here she describes a group of pieces called 'Regents heads':

> By 'Regents' I mean as in Regent's Park Zoo, in London, and all the portraits are loosely based on primates there – though as you can see, they are beyond most people's recognition now. The idea for the inverted pot shapes came from one of the Lyndenberg heads found in South Africa – the image socked me right between the eyes, and I knew immediately that I would use it.

These pieces have developed from a series of monkey heads made some years before. Originally it was a gentle piece of commentary on monkeys and apes, but it grew, via a study of monolithic heads, to an expression of consumption and sharp-toothed violence, culminating in the work entitled 'Scream'. Nigel Barley in *Smashing Pots* refers to the domestic use of an inverted pot in African culture as 'a denial of sexual favour'. Sue Halls' images of a sharp-toothed, grinning and leering mouth also cries of complaint, and there exists a true ambiguity of message: she captures this in an icon of avaricious denial, managing to overcome the apparent limitations of clay and to make a statement that is all the more powerful because it is made in a medium that is redolent of history and tradition. By blurring the distinctions between pot and figure she places her work in an arena that is specifically of ceramics – but she also wishes to escape what she perceives is the ghetto of craft objects. By making a distinction between vessel

'The red cook', Raku-fired, Michael Flynn.

'*Little* horror', thrown and assembled slabs, Raku-fired, Sue Halls.

'*Monkeys and apes*', thrown and assembled slabs, Raku-fired, Susan Halls.

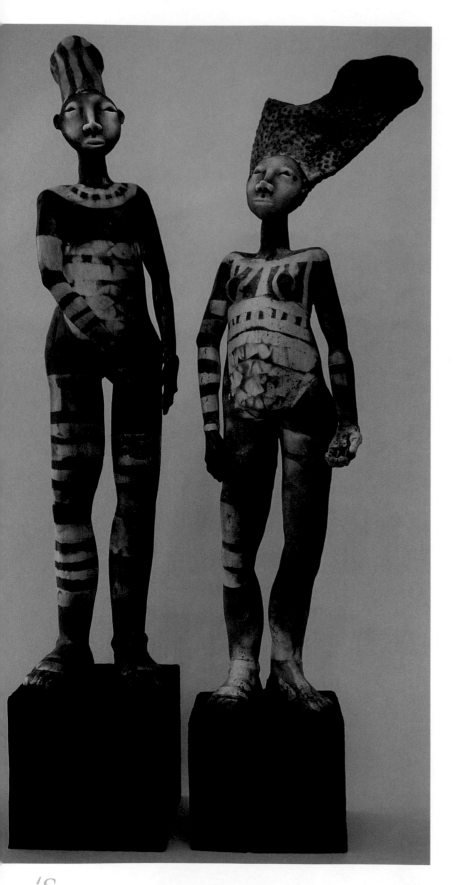

and figure she wishes to make her work itself distinctive:

> Pottery and vessels are generally easy on the eye. Looking at a 'pot' is a very immediate thing in terms of understanding, because any concept is conveniently camouflaged by an abstracted or minimalist reference to function – it is safe in its pottery-ness. Figurative work should be more demanding for the viewer – it should ask questions that require a lengthier contemplation. And it is precisely this time and attention that people are not prepared to invest. My work (at its best) is not decorative. I am not a story-teller or a caricaturist, and I don't offer humour on a plate.

The images are drawn from the world of animals, but instead of the apparent sweetness that infects much of the genre, her work speaks of aggression and blood, and conjures up an impression of inchoate violence brooding in dark recesses. She chooses Raku firing because it smudges and darkens even the gentlest of observations. Sometimes she has used a resist composed of clay masks applied after the bisque firing, against sawdust blackening; this can suggest the stripes of a zebra or the markings of a hyena (*see* page 52). At other times the painterly effect of red clay is contrasted with harsh carbon black to emphasize the sharpness of teeth. The predatory nature of the world (both natural and social) is always close at hand.

Sue Halls' pieces are ineluctably about clay and ceramic tradition. They are made using a combination of thrown elements and coiled sections, and they describe hollowness and trapped volume.

Sally Macdonell

Sally Macdonell creates female figures, wide-hipped and small-breasted, and adorned with grids and stripes that are imparted by smoke. Clothed only in their elaborate headpieces, they appear to be both vulnerable and at the same time assertive in their nakedness.

The pieces are potted hollow, using elements 'like brandy snaps'. She makes a point about this 'hollow skin' way of building, which seems to be trying to express the inner feelings of the women: 'When I model solid, my work does not say what I want it to, and this is why I prefer to model from the inside out.'

'Standing figures', sawdust-fired, Sally Macdonell.

An engobe is applied and fired to 1165°C. The pieces are wrapped in tape, then placed in a loose construction of bricks which acts as a kiln; they are submerged in sawdust and this is set alight, but it is allowed to smoulder for only ten minutes before Sally removes the pieces to check the degree of blackening. They are replaced until the coloration is judged to be right. Where the masking tape lay, the carbonization is partially resisted. Sally says: 'I use sawdust firings to give marks of experience on the surface of the figure. The fire/smoke leaves its own unique fingerprint.'

Ian Gregory

Ian Gregory hints at his purpose when he talks about his work: 'One of the goals towards which I strive when I am manipulating clay is to work from the creative union of conscious and unconscious thought.' Ian's work is about memory and possibility: as he works, experiences dimly recalled are reinterpreted as he fashions the clay form. As he states:

> These surfaces and tensions I search for are ambivalent, reflecting the passage of time, the material, the maker's hand in combination with the final metamorphosis of fire.

Ian is trying to capture that fleeting quality of 'the moment', when the figure, be it animal or human, is 'frozen' – although his intention is not to make a three-dimensional snapshot photograph:

> It is an instant stolen from the chronology of one thing moving into another. In our memories there are visual things that are only half known; there is a lot of amorphous junk, as well as specific information about an animal or person that we do know. What I am trying to do is to capture that archetypal image, and not to create 'jam for the eyeballs'.

He quotes from T.S. Eliot's poem *Four Quartets*, which geographically is centred near his part of Somerset:

> Time present and time past
> Are both perhaps present in time future
> And time future contained in time past.
> If all time is eternally present
> All time is unredeemable.

'*Man in the moon*', *Raku-fired, Ian Gregory.*

Eliot's poetry represents a transition to a secular society – while he was a committed 'high churchman', he is also the poet of despair, expressing the ending of certainty in the world. A person of committed religious beliefs may talk of trying to capture the soul of his subjects; Gregory says: 'Nowadays there is little need to make Sacred Art any more, since we do not work from religious convictions in the same way as earlier artists. They, however humble, gave their objects meaning and visual poise, and imbued them with an intense feeling of inner spirituality.'

Ian Gregory uses '… the process of Raku and low temperature salt, which places very special demands on me as a maker – the materials used become a battlefield for the elements of earth, fire and water'. He makes a plea for a place for pottery at the end of the millennium: 'One of the contemporary roles for ceramics is that it continues to provide aesthetic consolation, and to enrich daily life on a domestic scale.'

To process his work Ian Gregory has built fifteen fire-brick plinths in his kiln shed, each with a covering of sand and ceramic fibre, so that each piece can be built on a plinth and fired without being moved. The large figures are built over an armature of chicken wire; this is covered in paper clay, and soil-heating cables are threaded through the work – up or around a leg, into the body cavity and out of an orifice – to help the drying process; this will also prevent the work freezing in the winter. Wrapped in polythene the humidity will equalize, and when condensation no longer forms on the plastic, it is dry enough to bisque. A flat-pack kiln is quickly built around a piece and the burners and gas connected to it. The chicken wire is burnt out in the bisque firing by a long soak at 1100°C; the wire melts or it can be brushed out (*see* pages 65 and 66).

Emma Rodgers

The development in Rodgers' work has gradually shown a shift away from verisimilitude; she is no longer merely creating a copy of an animal, but making pieces whose currency is analogies and correspondences. She is an artist who aspires to capture the very simplest, yet deepest, of qualities. She chiefly works on a small scale and often with domestic themes; in her work there is a power and tension in the poses that makes the work transcend the mundane and enables her to recreate the essence of the animal that she is studying. She says: 'I aim to capture the moment. To achieve this I do a large amount of visual research including film, photography and drawing. Sketching is particularly important as it provides me with a greater understanding of form. The translation of drawn marks provides ideas that could not flow from photographs alone.'

Thus her work is actually shaped by the means she has chosen to record her source of inspira-

'Hare', sawdust-fired, Emma Rodgers.

tion: if sketching, for example, she is able to introduce qualities that move the piece far away from pure representation – it develops as a dialogue between drawing and expression in clay, in a search for correspondences – so a jagged line in ink is reinterpreted as torn clay, and an arc of soft pencil becomes a rolled clay edge. Also the energy of the animal and the tautness of its pose is conveyed by a similar distortion in the clay itself – she will stretch the clay, often to the point at which it splits and breaks. This led her to an essential part of her style, which is 'statement by omission': through leaving out certain of the animals' features and focussing attention on the 'negative spaces within the form', she discovered that she was better able to describe the animal, and suggest the spirit that animates it. The hollowness of a piece, and being able to see through the walls, makes the trapped volume a significant aspect of the work. It can act symbolically, like the empty inside space of a vessel, as a metaphoric container for our thoughts.

Her subject matter is various, and the choice is mainly the result of personal experience. Thus she deals with a world with which we are familiar, with pet cats and rabbits – and yet she captures the feeling of an ancestral feline whose savagery is only temporarily tamed, or wild rabbits and hares successfully colonizing the land, ancient symbols of fecundity. There is also a harshness in her treatment of surface that implies a wild, free spirit forcing its way out of the straitjacket of the 'civilized' world.

She has also observed and commented on the human condition, producing figurative work that considers the human animal in its own, culturally determining environment; she believes that the ways in which women are viewed by their peers is conditioned by contemporary media and the art from the past.

> Observing women in changing-rooms, I found it amusing how we pose, preen, squash and squeeze ourselves, whilst looking in the mirror. … Whilst building one particular piece, I stretched and tore the clay to give it stronger definition, and accidentally tore off too much clay on one of the breasts. However, when viewed from various angles it still had the illusion of form, so I decided to develop this idea and incorporate it to a greater degree in my work … moreover, at the British Museum I found myself increasingly drawn to the heavily decayed pieces, as I felt they were very strong and did not *need* the missing elements.

'W*oman', sawdust-fired, Emma Rodgers.*

She reinterprets the attrition of time by ripping and tearing the clay, and the work is finally resolved by leaving some parts incomplete.

Her most recent work incorporates a critique of the relationship between man and animals. It is also about the experience of being a watcher. The zoo is the most exposed, and one of the least private, environments for animals, and may be considered analogous to the artist who exists through observing his subjects, thereby invading their privacy. Furthermore the keeping of primates as pets, trapped in a zoo or working the seaside resorts as a gimmick, is shown to be ridiculous. Rodgers uses found materials to particular purpose, namely to heighten the sense of animals being exploited and oppressed; they suggest parts of the body, but they are also meant to be a comment on the curbing of the free animal spirit by human intrusion.

This alienation of the animal world is further investigated by placing them in a referential ceramic context; in one particular piece of two monkeys, Rodgers says:

I wanted the monkeys to work as a pair, reminiscent of Staffordshire dogs on a mantelpiece. The roller-skates, like the clothes they wear, are superficial apart from the function of performing for our pleasure … The next influence on my work was a toy dog with a spring stomach. I felt that introducing the spring into my monkeys would not only make them more like toys, but it also resembled a rib-cage.

A piece is built from a variety of white clays and porcelain, and it grows by the accumulation of clay modules – a hybrid of *patties* and *brandy-snaps*. It is bisque-fired, and then painted in a style based on Japanese ink painting techniques: first Rodgers applies a watery underglaze using large soft brushes; then, in order to introduce into the piece her own drawn marks derived from the sketching process, she monoprints black earthenware glaze in specific areas to represent the lines in her actual drawings. The piece is refired to 1100°C; this makes it hard enough to survive, yet it is still sufficiently porous to absorb carbon from the smoke firing. In order to suggest light falling across the camouflage fur of her subjects, Emma uses smudges of colour derived from materials that give only slight staining from carbon; thus she may burn a little sawdust mixed with magazine pages around the work, the sawdust providing soft greys and the magazine paper giving hints of blue.

Contemporary Responses: The Processial

Clay

Although clay is obviously the medium used by all the artists in the book, there are some for whom it is also the subject of their work. This focus can extend to the processes by which the work comes into being. In a sense it could encompass all the potters mentioned here, though only a few take it to the extreme.

Verity Eastwood

Verity's work brings to mind geology: it is not so much a statement about hollowness and the space contained within a vessel or form, but about mass and solidity – it is about presence and presentness. There are allusions to vessels, but essentially these pieces are about walls and structure, and not about pots. First the clay is built up layer upon layer into a solid mass, in the same way that a river might tumble clays and rocks together, compressing them by force and gravity. Under the ostensible lack of purpose there is a powerful sense of order in her work, the motivation being her religious beliefs; it is a structure that is woven into its very texture. Furthermore, when she describes her creative methods, it is clear that it is all a painstaking process of hand-building:

I laminate widely differing clay bodies, slips and grogs – anything from brick clay to porcelain – into large chunks of solid clay which are then carved, torn and worked into container/vessel forms. My painstaking layering of clay builds up a structure within which literally anything might happen at later stages. There is a constant balancing between controlling the materials, and 'letting them go'. I know what clays I have put into a piece, but I can't always predict how they will reveal their characters through the making, drying and firing process.

Once the mass of clay is established, it is left so that its moisture content has a chance to equalize; then begins the process of attrition:

The ways in which different clays react together, the speed at which they'll dry, where they'll lift or fracture, and what 'strata' I'll bring to light when I cut, tear or burnish them … all of these are relatively unknown, and unknowable quantities. I have a 'direction' at the start of a piece, but not complete knowledge, or even control of the process. The best pieces are those which embrace this unpredictability. Perhaps there are, after all, parallels here with the *laissez faire* Raku way of thinking.

pottery that led me to specialize in low temperature clays and firing techniques. I saw that you can get such wonderful richness and varied depth of surface just with the raw clay and slips, that somehow I never got any further down the glazes path. The low-fire processes seem to suit my mentality as well – or rather they constantly challenge my control-freak tendencies, just as my 'making' process does. There is something rather humbling in surrendering a piece of precious work to the whims of burning banana skins.

By examining each piece of work so critically she can view it objectively; she can also investigate the ideas that led to its inception, and perhaps get a sense of its destination, too. Clay as dug clay is a central theme. By coating areas of the work with terra sigillatas made from found clays, she emphasizes even more strongly the connection to the Earth:

I started working in this way on my degree course at Wolverhampton. In fact it was not Raku, but my study of earlier African and Ancient Greek

The firing is a visible fusing, literally, of the clay but also, conceptually, of the ideas: a 'bringing together', in which the scars of sawdust smoke smudge the discreet layers and unify the piece.

On first sight my work is far removed from traditional Raku ware, but although it may appear to be very different, perhaps the mentality with which I approach it is not so very distant from the traditional Eastern way of thinking and working with clay.

'Laminated vessels', found clays, sawdust-fired, Verity Eastwood. (Photograph by Dave Jones.)

*S*traw structure,
sawdust-fired, Polly
Macpherson.

*S*traw structure, sawdust-fired, Polly Macpherson.

Polly Macpherson

Polly has evolved a methodology for making her work that ignores many of the proprieties of ceramic. The permanence of the pieces is not an issue if this will compromise the aesthetic. The pieces celebrate the after-effects of combustion and the friable three-dimensional images of what is no longer there: the illusion is of straw and hay, but in fact it has fired away. It is a natural material turned into a solid, hard form.

The pieces are created from combustible materials, particularly straw, dipped in clay casting slip. The apparent disorder is given a struc-

ture and form by assembling the pieces in a plaster mould or on plaster batts. 'I am doing a lot of work with the rectangular shape, which I find quite claustrophobic.' These pieces are bisque-fired before being smoked in sawdust. In fact the notion of creating order out of chaos is now an established motif in her practice:

The notion of matrix and the ways in which order can be imposed by structuring and arrangement has become a major theme in my ceramic work … Also I find the forms need the very subtle colouring which the sawdust firing provides. I do a lot of work after firing, re-oxidizing the forms with a blowtorch. Furthermore I really like the fact that you can always change your mind and take the form out of the firing there and then. This has a lot to do with the fact that I like to keep my options open at all times.

Pam Salter

Pam Salter conceptualizes her work in terms of the following contradictory elements, in which one can perceive a sense of progress through opposition. She poses statements and questions as arcane as a Zen koan:

> My work is made on the wheel but is rarely about round forms.
>
> Its roots are firmly in nature, but hopefully it does not imitate.

> I strive to incorporate so much, but also so little. (Why should less be more?)

This riddling style informs her reflections on process, where there is planning, and no planning. The work grows out of a familiarity with technique that creates a sense of easy accomplishment – as if the pieces are coming into existence by themselves. There is the evocation of the intimate parts of plants or sea creatures, parts which are normally kept sheathed and hidden from view, but which suddenly appear to burst through their concealing skin and parade in their folded convolutions.

Salter's creation of form, and likewise her mark-making, derive their vocabulary from the potter's wheel:

> I am fascinated by the mechanics and the processes of throwing, the plasticity of clay, and

Thrown form, terra sigillata, *saggar-fired, Pam Salter.*

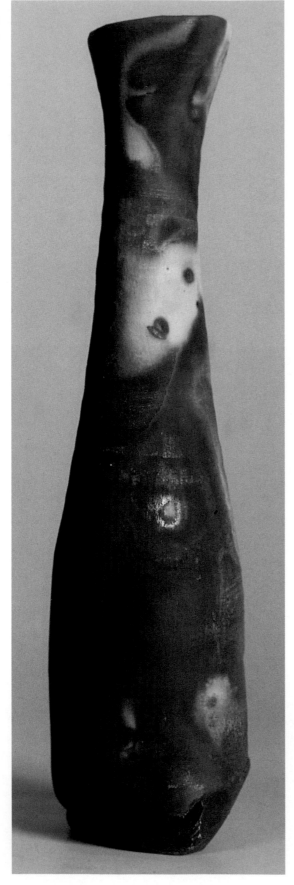

Vase, low temperature salt, 18in (46cm) high, Paul Soldner.

taking it to its structural limits. I search for solutions to questions of contained and manipulated space, and of organic growth. The aim is for a structured simplicity, exploring through an evolving enquiry. I attempt to capture the essence of references derived from the nuances of drawing with clay in its fluid state.

The pieces are bisque-fired; after this a fine coat of iron oxide is applied, and then layers of white terra sigillata. They are then fired in a saggar with sawdust to approximately 750°C. The pots can be re-fired a number of times until they have developed the appropriate level of carbonization.

Paul Soldner

Paul Soldner is an artist whose work is inextricably bound up in the history of Raku. He is one of the chief popularisers and re-inventors of the technique, and his work seems to focus on *process* in a very central way. Largely ignorant of the generation of Japanese Raku practitioners, he spliced this exciting technique that he had read about in Leach's *A Potter's Book* together with an analogy in clay terms to what was happening in abstract expressionist painting.

> The speed at which Raku could be made allowed spontaneity and opened the way to the creation of new shapes that capitalised on the new freedom from the rigid control of the older utilitarian high-temperature tradition (of Japanese tea-ceremony vessels).

Soldner's own work normally develops from wheel-thrown pieces, which are then *happened* – slung on the floor, trampled underfoot and beaten – and then very mindfully presented. The resulting textures are carefully preserved under a thin vapour glaze of salt, a haze of metal salts or blackened starkly with carbonized sawdust. The figure which used to play a central part in the iconography of his decoration is now hinted at in the visceral structures of the form that result from the process of making. His most recent work is high-fired in a wood kiln. It continues to embody the concept of 'Rakuness' that he defines as 'somehow so apparently easy that we forget for the moment the discipline … and the focussed dedication that made it possible … it transcends its own process and uplifts the observer and gives meaning to human existence'.

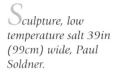

Sculpture, low temperature salt 39in (99cm) wide, Paul Soldner.

Sculpture, high temperature wood fired 25in (63.5cm) wide, Paul Soldner.

Surface

Raku and low-temperature firings are capable of creating such seductive surfaces that this could be a section into which one could place many potters. This is a selection of artists who make a serious investigation into surface qualities and use that outer skin of the pot in a referential way.

Tim Andrews

Tim Andrews trained with David Leach, the son of Bernard Leach; he wrote one of the most recent books on Raku. He felt himself imprisoned working within the Anglo-Japanese tradition '… for the most part regurgitating someone else's ideas. The result was a growing dissatisfaction with the work, together with something of an identity crisis.' He started to work in Raku as a result of a search for an 'untaught' area of ceramics, unconstrained by knowledge and tradition; but now he feels trapped again: 'The word "Raku" was a convenient title for people to get hold of at first; now it only restricts the perception of the extremely wide range of low-fired work that is around.' One might dispute this, and it could be maintained that the use of the word 'Raku' has actually extended its range, and that now it encompasses an even wider embrace of ceramic processes: the creativity of Raku artists is extended by using the word 'Raku' to conjure up all those ghosts from the past and join them to current usage.

Tim recognizes that the constraints demanded of him in working within his own interpretation of the Raku medium brought a certain rigour, but in fact he views this as '… the liberating factor, rather in the same way that some poets find their freedom within a rhyming structure – the self-enforced discipline encourages a more creative response': it acts as a creative boundary.

Tim Andrews' work is '… a variation on a particular form': this has involved throwing pots on the wheel, many with an involuted, introverted rim. They are finished using the 'resist slip' decoration technique, featuring a form of drawing through a glaze containing bubbles (*see* page 51).

'*Tall form*', *thrown and Raku-fired with resist slip, Tim Andrews. (Photograph by Sam Bailey.)*

'*Mosaic bowl*',
*Raku-fired, Melanie
Brown.*

*Raku-fired vessels
with gilded interiors,
Emma Johnstone.*

Melanie Brown

Melanie Brown's work deals with images composed of fragments lying on top of perfectly thrown bowls, with an area for containment and a wide rim for decoration. The inspiration for the borders comes from research into mosaic. By drawing on the geometry of pattern she has developed a mode of decoration that enhances the Far Eastern ceramic forms that are the basis of her repertoire, while Raku firing conjures up the antique, with its patinated surfaces. She recreates the gaps in the tesserae by drawing in latex, which is peeled off before firing, to ensure there are no traces of glaze left where the pot should read black.

Emma Johnstone

Emma Johnstone makes unglazed, double-walled vessels; these are thrown upside-down on the wheel, as one dome enclosing another. After trimming, the pot is bisque-fired and then the piece is prepared for a Raku firing. No glaze is used: the thermal shock to the pot creates the crackle pattern by fracturing the clay body with hairline cracks; after the firing and secondary reduction this crackle pattern is obscured by the superficial

Raku-fired bowl, Karin Östberg.

Raku-fired box, Karin Östberg.

deposit of carbon. However, the stain penetrates the cracks in the clay, and these are revealed by grinding back the wide rims. The pots are then soaked in water to eliminate dust, and abraded using graded metal grinding discs. They are finished with fine grades of wet and dry (carborundum) paper. At this stage the 'tooth' of the clay is revealed, and the choice of coarse or fine grogs in the clay creates a surface texture. Finally the interiors are gilded with gold, platinum or copper leaf.

Karin Östberg

Karin Östberg, a potter from Norway, creates clay objects that speak about impermanence. She makes the innate fragility of the pieces a distinctive quality, and has devised a building technique which leads to an expressive and seemingly archaic surface; this is enhanced by the Raku firing process.

The work is made by hollowing out a solid form and then slapping clay onto the simple structure to create a granular surface; cracks are a part of its aesthetic.

After bisque firing, washes of soluble salts such as copper sulphate and ferric chloride are poured over the pieces; they are then placed in the kiln. On removal, the red-hot pots are either directly smoked in sawdust, or more of these washes are poured onto the hot clay, before secondary reduction.

NOTE: Extreme care must be exercised when handling these materials which are toxic, and a rebreathing face mask should be worn.

John Wheeldon

John Wheeldon disavows the Anglo-Oriental tradition of Leach, and speaks of utilizing the indigenous pottery skills of England, in particular the slip-trailing tradition; he would also use the tools developed by pottery workers in Stoke-on-Trent – for instance roulettes.

His Raku work developed while he was engaged in decoration with geometrically printed lustres on a black 'basalt' body. Commercial lustres have their reduction material already mixed in, and can be affected by Raku firing. Raku firing and secondary reduction now provide the black ground and the lustrous surfaces for which he is searching.

Applying latex resist to a bowl (top) and removing latex resist from a bowl after spraying with copper matt glaze (bottom), John Wheeldon.

*R*aku-fumed vessel,
John Wheeldon.

Fire

Some potters have grown through Raku and associated earthenware methodologies to make fire the main focus of their work. Thus the performance element in Raku, or the scarring of clay by flame, becomes the central subject for these artists.

Sebastian Blackie

Sebastian Blackie compares ceramics with gardening: the work develops and accumulates organically, and then the unsuccessful pieces are weeded out. He also celebrates the planned accidental happening: although one may be engaged in a very specific search, if something

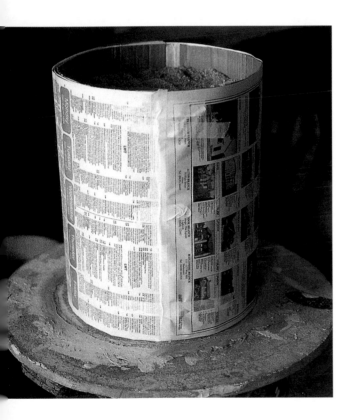

interesting crops up, then it can be used. He describes a continuum between 'topiary potters' who plan very precisely, and 'cottage garden potters' who allow things to happen.

Methods of building clay have developed so that the fire itself appears to be captured in the actual vessel. Pots were fired in paper clay saggars, and these were pierced strategically so that in the firing, air could penetrate and leave a trace

on the surface of the carbonized clay where it had re-oxidized to red. These swirls echo the traditions of ceramic as varied as Greek red and black figureware, and Beaker pots made as funerary urns thousands of years ago.

Blackie has gone on to make complex and very organized 'baskets' of wrapped and rolled paper. These exhibit in their regularity a high degree of control, and a recognizably traditional 'craft skill': true to the original method, clay is pushed onto the inside surface of this structure and forms the basis of an apparently crude clay vessel which nevertheless carries traces of this organized

Pierced saggar built of cardboard and clay slip, Sebastian Blackie (left).

Vessel showing re-oxidized red mark from air directed through a hole in pierced saggar, Sebastian Blackie.

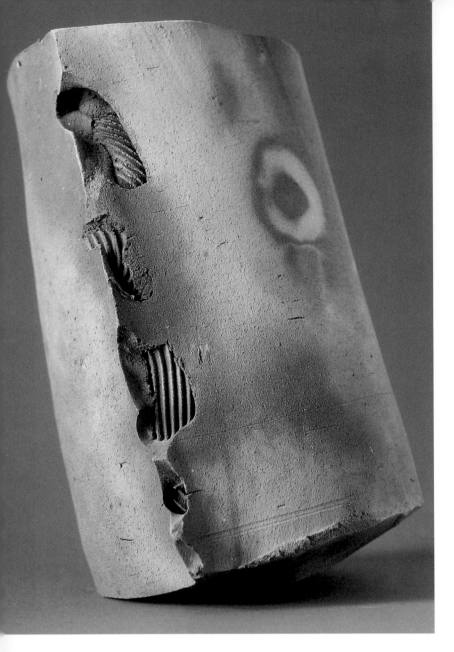

*P*ot fired in sawdust-filled, pierced saggar, Sebastian Blackie.

*R*aku-fired house form, Nina Hole (right).

preparation. The basket and clay are carefully dried, and then they are set on fire, normally assisted in a kiln; when finished, they still carry traces of these ordered marks. This work recalls the vessels or baskets putatively used by Neolithic man to transport fire from one place to another.

Nina Hole

Nina Hole is a Danish potter who has worked in Raku since 1970. However, she has developed her technique so that now she is producing work of monumental scale: she calls these pieces 'Sculpturekiln', and each is a self-firing structure. She explains how Raku methodology enabled her to process her ideas quickly, and gave her the scope to experiment with clay and firing; she was also attracted to the notion of clay and firing taking centre stage in a celebratory community activity, another idea which had its roots in the Raku practice of many people taking part in a firing, thereby ritualizing the process of making and burning.

Hole works with Debra English, and together they co-ordinate a team of helpers, drawn from the locality where she has been commissioned to work; these all assist in the 'performance' associated with each firing. References to architecture underpin Nina's work: 'For many years I have been working with the house form to express my thoughts. My sculptures are built consciously using negative space as openings for light to come through; and by combining clay with other materials such as glass I have added both light and lightness to the heaviness of the clay.'

The firing of the piece takes place at night, and is positively theatrical. And when the fibre blanket is removed to reveal the red-hot Sculpturekiln, one could say that an immediate parallel is drawn with the Raku experience of removing the kiln sur-

rounding a pot. With the Sculpturekiln the whole purpose and objective is fire, and it is this focus on an essential part of the ceramic process that calls to mind the experience of the earliest Raku firings. Finally, as the dawn breaks and exhaustion descends (and that is only in the audience), the participants enact a ceremony, which may be seen as a celebration of the 'rebirth of Raku'; as if to 'sanctify' post-firing reduction, sawdust is thrown onto the piece by the helpers. Nina recalls: 'It was almost like a dance around the sculpture. It was a beautiful moment; and each time the sawdust hit the piece it would flare up and a new energy was sparked in all of us.'

Ray Rogers

Ray Rogers is a New Zealander, though he is based in Australia; he travels the world enthusiastically demonstrating pit firing. He coils and

Pit-fired 'Layered form', Ray Rogers.

throws large, smooth vessels that are the ideal canvas for collecting the marks of firing. The pots are bisque-fired, and then they are placed in a trench in the ground, surrounded by volatile metal salts, covered by wood and ignited. The fire deposits traces of its passage on the work leaving vivid flashes of colour.

Michael Scheuermann

Michael Scheuermann trained in Germany as a stonemason; he then studied sculpture and ceramics at Wolverhampton University. It is therefore hardly surprising that his work exhibits a fascination with stone and ceramic. From time immemorial clay and sandstone have shared an existence as sedimentary deposits – yet after all these millions of years, one short firing can change them utterly. Michael says:

Clay and stone are related in their geology, and their functional use in history goes back to the first vessels and shelters of mankind. They are both the traditional, basic materials of sculpture, and I find their use very appropriate to catch a moment within a piece and thus to create an awareness of the ceaseless stream of other moments. I try to achieve this by fusing them together in various ways to obtain different forms.

The piece 'On line' is about sandstone, clay, ceramic and fire. A length of coping stone was split in half lengthways; a section was then cut from the rock, clay was inserted, and a line was cut with a grinder through both materials, thus uniting them. A line of low-melting Raku glaze was placed as a powder in the groove, and the piece was then fired in about ten hours, or until the temperature was high enough to melt the glaze. The clay fires and changes to stone; the green sandstone is oxidized to red, and firemarks stain the edges. The

'On line', fired sandstone, clay and glaze, Michael Scheuermann. (See page 76 for a picture of the kiln.)

glaze becomes fluid, and then sets. Finally the coping is reunited with its Siamese twin. The effects of the firing are traumatic: it is a dramatic symbol of permanence and change.

Hazel Thomson

Hazel Thomson uses blackness and the fragility of her materials – paper and clay – in both a metaphorical and a metaphysical way:

> All clay embraces the shadows of the past … Metal rusts away, cloth rots, yet the museum vaults are full of shards of pots. For clay, once fired, has a permanence like no other material. Therefore my quest has been to create clay which has an implicit solidity, but could be crumbled away by hand. A single, paper-thin clay is destructible to the slightest movement. However, layers of paper-thin clay gain a strength which can prove to be deceptive. And these provide the boundary which 'serves to indicate the limit'. It is only in the testing, only in the intrusion that we discover whether or not we have come up against a movable barrier.

As a student, Hazel worked continuously within the field of low-temperature ceramics, exploring the possibilities offered by the darkness of carbon. Firstly it was within the realms of Raku and post-firing reduction, but then, as her fascination with blackness developed, she examined other ways of dealing with the apparent absence of light. Her method was to make mini clay saggars, seal the combustible material within, and then fire them in a gas kiln; after firing, they were cut open with a 'diamond saw'. This left a sharp, harsh edge – a perfect foil, representing control, to the unrestrained combustion and extreme reduction of the clay within. The saggars themselves became the work.

One of the best materials found to manufacture the saggars was paper clay (after a suggestion by Sebastian Blackie). Paper can be as much as 50 per cent china clay – this is the nebulous residue left in the grate after burning a sheet of paper. Thus paper is a combination of clay and combustibles that simply needs strengthening with more clay. Thomson eventually found that these saggars became objects in their own right, largely because the paper that was originally only a part of their make-up, actually became another subject of the firing investigations, and a significant part of the work (*see also* page 56).

*S*aggar-fired ceramic 'Footsteps on shadows', Hazel Thomson.

6 Away from a Standard

Contemporary Raku and low-firing practice is both modern, and also ancient. In the nineteenth century the French poet and aesthetician Baudelaire made the distinction between permanent qualities – those that can last for all time – and transitory values, which will give us pleasure and delight for but a day. He wrote in *The Painter in Modern Life*:

> By modernity I mean the ephemeral, the fugitive, the contingent, the half of art whose other half is the eternal and the immutable.

So if we look at the traditional aesthetic distinction between form and content, then we might say that objects that have a message to communicate have but a short (ephemeral) life, whilst communication *per se* still remains relevant to its audience. This pertinence can wane as the times change.

Other, more abstract expression may have a more contemplative function. It is a radical version of this distinction, between objects that are made for all time and those that speak to us now, that is implied by Bernard Leach in his writings. In the second edition of *A Potter's Book* – in which he told the story of Raku – he also wrote a new chapter entitled 'Towards a Standard'. This was written during World War II, a period of transition and rapidly changing values. In order to establish a standard whereby contemporary works might be measured against past values of excellence, Leach selected the Sung (or Song) bowl. For him these pots represented an (apparently) unpretentious landmark in restrained high-temperature glazing, created by Chinese potters about a thousand years ago. As *A Potter's Book* was the first primer for craft potters it was hugely influential, and the ideal of the restrained Chinese pot was blindly pursued by many British and American potters during the last fifty years – this is despite Leach's insistence that it was the *spirit* of the work that was to be emulated: it was not meant to be the slavish making of copies. Leach describes this yardstick:

> Accepting the 'Sung' standard means the use, so far as is possible, of natural materials, in the endeavour to obtain the best qualities of body and glaze; in throwing it means a striving towards unity, spontaneity and simplicity of form, and in general the subordination of all attempts at technical cleverness to straightforward, unselfconscious workmanship.

This is an aesthetic tenet of 'truth to materials' that echoes Henry Moore and Barbara Hepworth, but also imposes the Japanese notion of artisanal anonymity in the production of functional pottery.

Leach was writing at a time when canons of work were being established. In the field of literature F.R. Leavis compiled lists of key texts (re-evaluation), and in painting Panovsky and Gombrich proposed new standards of excellence by which all other achievement can be measured. In British ceramic circles fashions changed slowly, but gradually the taste for the burnt browns of an autumnal palette abated, and the 1970s saw the burgeoning of experiment in colour and surface. These pieces were often hand-built and non-functional.

Also at this time ideas concerning the nature of craft education that had originated in the Bauhaus were becoming highly influential; this was particularly the case in art schools which had taken over the main part of the education of potters, as the apprentice system broke down. The Bauhaus philosophy also suggested an alternative view of the relationship of craftsman and industry. By contrast with Ruskin, Morris and

Leach, the possibilities offered by the machine were perceived neutrally, and not as necessarily alienating. As such it was a code for an urban population. The Bauhaus philosophy encouraged a freedom in thinking, and most importantly in Britain, it encouraged a looking outside of Leach's canon of the ideal Chinese pot. The aesthetic of the Bauhaus is also one of restraint.

By contrast, in the 1970s, new attitudes to clay surface were imported with the developing interest in American painting. Apprentices are relatively isolated in their rural workshops, whereas in an art school the departments are often only a flight of steps apart. Communication opens up the possibilities for influence, and at this time clay artists absorbed the influence of Expressionist painting, which celebrated accident and a spontaneous attack on surface. This, combined with the Funk ceramics movement in America, which celebrated the transitory and embraced a gaudy palette of colour, laid the foundations for the rise of Raku and low fire in the seventies.

In the making of, and particularly in the firing of, ceramics Raku has been a by-word for 'experimentation' and 'letting things happen' for over thirty years, and Western Raku potters have exuberantly twisted the processes of building and glazing to create a new aesthetic. The toxic Raku glazes and porous sawdust-fired pots could not be functional, and therefore much of the thrust of the work has been towards metaphoric vessels and statements in clay about fire. Western Raku started as an exuberant experiment. As a low-temperature firing methodology, with its concomitant predisposition to bright colour, it was ideally suited to be one of the main techniques to depose the high-temperature aesthetic code that was the legacy of Bernard Leach.

A number of important strands in the development of contemporary Raku and low fire have been pulled together over the last half century. One strand in this weaving is found in the writings of Michael Cardew. Of all the students who worked and studied with Bernard Leach, Cardew was the one who subsequently was the most influential. It was Cardew's attempt to export the Sung standard that in a sense also disproved it as a universal code. Leach brought back from Japan a knowledge and reverence for craft stoneware, and this knowledge and respect was inculcated into Michael Cardew; so when Cardew left England to run a pottery in Abuja, in Nigeria, he took with him the secrets of high temperature glazes that had been perfected by

Hamada and Tomimoto who were both working at the St Ives pottery.

Cardew spent many years trying to impose his knowledge on both the indigenous materials and on the population he had been sent to train. This was an importation of skills accustomed to dealing with the alien materials found in Asia and Britain, and for a long while he made no attempt to look at the skills and methodologies that had grown up around the locally dug materials. As Cardew related in his more recent book *A Pioneer Potter*, the emphasis on stoneware (and the accompanying insistence on the Sung bowl as the apogee of ceramic attainment) had nothing to do with the culture and accomplishments of the African population – and it also showed that it was foolish, if not downright arrogant, to try to impose a single, universal standard of excellence. The pots that he made using locally sourced clays failed because they melted or cracked – they had been fired to an inappropriate temperature.

What Cardew brought back to England was not just a sense of personal fallibility, an indictment of cultural imperialism, or even just a critique of the over-reaching ambition of Leach's 'gospel' of the Chinese and Japanese high-firing aesthetic, but the notion that it was also possible to achieve qualities of surface at non-vitrifying temperatures. In order to put forward these ideas he invited Ladi Kwali, the great African coil potter, to visit Europe, and her influence came to be felt at the same time as Mediterranean ceramics were re-establishing themselves. It is quite apparent that a cup from the palaces of Knossos, or a Cypriot water jar, or a Beaker burial urn is easily the equal of the Asian achievements – and suddenly it was possible to view hand-built clay objects in the same light as the Sung and Ming dynasty vessels. Moreover in the bonfire-fired pots of Africa the effects of the combustion can be tangibly seen in the body of a piece – a more intimate expression of the natural forces that create a clay object are shown in the naked clay of an African cooking pot than would ever be possible in the 'super-subtle' properties of a porcelain bowl.

In parallel with these events taking place in Europe, the potters of North America were investigating the vestiges of the indigenous cultures that had been displaced by the arrival of the European. From the 1950s in America a real interest developed in the simple firing technologies of the native potters. These technologies were the product of ancient traditions, and when this awareness was combined with the rationale emerging from the American interpretation of Raku, it was possible for a new aesthetic to be developed which celebrated the nuances of marking through firing.

To begin with it was like froth on the sea, and there was a depth to these ancient traditions that we, new practitioners, were quite ignorant of. Although Bernard Leach returned from Japan with a reverential attitude towards much Oriental ceramic, he seems, nonetheless, to have been less interested in that most sophisticated of aesthetics embedded in 'tea ceremony'.

Nowadays, Raku is no longer regarded as *just* a fun, party-time or crowd-pleasing sideline, but it has now come centre stage and is regarded as one of the main methodologies for processing ideas in clay. The move in ceramic aesthetics from a modernist sensibility (with its notion of an ideal pot to which a potter should aspire) and the post-modern world, with its multiplicity of styles and effects, has been driven, in part, by Raku and its associated low-temperature firing techniques. What I have charted in contemporary expression seems to me to be a display of increasing control over chance effects. It has also created an environment that has allowed a daring in the firing of unconventional materials and to a position where firing itself has become a goal and the actual performance of firing a kiln an endpoint of expression.

The link from the future returns us to the past and we contemporary practitioners benefit enormously from the profundity of the traditions that underpin Raku practice, in the ways in which they inform our thinking about clay, process and firing.

Bibliography

Andrews, T., *Raku* (A & C Black, London, 1994).

Bachelard, G., *The Psychoanalysis of Fire* (Quartet Books, London, 1987).

Barley, N., *Smashing Pots. Feats of Clay from Africa* (British Museum Press, London, 1994).

Branfman, S., *Raku, A Practical Approach* (A & C Black, London, 1991).

Burns, Marla, *Ceramic Histories.*

Byers, I., *The Complete Potter, Raku* (B.T. Batsford Ltd., 1990).

Cardew, M., *Pioneer Pottery* (Longmans, London, 1969).

Cardew, M., *A Pioneer Potter.*

Castile, R., *Chanoyu: Japanese Tea Ceremony* (Weatherhill, New York).

Hamer, F. & J., *The Potter's Illustrated Dictionary of Materials and Techniques* (A & C Black, London).

Hirsch, R. and Tyler, *Raku* (Pitman, 1975).

Kichizaemon Raku XV. Exhibition catalogue and essay.

Leach, B., *A Potter's Book* (Faber, London, 1973).

Leach, B., *Kenzan and his Tradition* (Faber, London, 1966).

Levi-Strauss, C., *The Raw and the Cooked.*

Levi-Strauss, C., *The Savage Mind* (Penguin, London, 1966).

Piepenburg, *Raku Pottery* (Macmillan, New York, 1972).

Rawson, P., *Ceramics* (University of Pennsylvania Press, 1984).

Rhodes, D., *Clay and Glazes for the Potter* (A & C Black, London, 1975).

Riegger H., *Primitive Pottery* (Van Nostrand, New York, 1972).

Sanders, H., *The World of Japanese Ceramics* (Kodansha, Tokyo, 1967).

Soshitsu Sen XV, *Tea Life, Tea Mind* (Weatherhill, New York, 1989).

Suzuki, D.T., *Chanoyu* (Japan Society).

Waal, E., *Bernard Leach* (Tate Gallery pub., London, 1998).

Wilson, R., *Inside Japanese Ceramics* (Weatherhill, New York, 1991).

Publications

American Ceramics, 15 west 44th Street, New York, NY 10036, USA.

Ceramics Art and Perception, 35 William St., Paddington, Sidney, NSW2012, Australia.

Ceramics Monthly, Professional Publications, Inc., Box 12448, Columbus, Ohio, 43212, USA.

Ceramic Review, 21 Carnaby St., London, W1V 1PH, UK.

Studio Pottery, 15 Magdalene Road, Exeter, EX2 4TA, UK.

Index

Bold entries are for artists featured in the book.